STREAMLINED DRI

TEN AMAZING UNBUILT AUTOMOBILE DESIGNS

1916–1939

Jared A. Zichek

RETROMECHANIX PRODUCTIONS

First published in the United States of America in 2017 by Jared A. Zichek, 12615 North Wildwood Point Road, Hauser, Idaho 83854

E-mail: editor@retromechanix.com

ISBN: 978-0-9968754-2-4

www.retromechanix.com

CONTENTS

INTRODUCTION

Automotive engineers have produced countless preliminary designs and unrealized projects since Karl Benz created the first true automobile in 1885. Most of these concepts never left the drawing board because they were superseded by better designs or financial resources were lacking to develop them. The majority of these studies were likely discarded, with a small percentage being retained in company archives or the personal files of the designers and engineers who worked on them. Some were novel enough to be patented, their drawings and descriptions being preserved at the patent office. Of these surviving projects, there are a select few which are so striking or unorthodox that they—in my opinion, at least—deserve to be examined in greater detail.

The automotive designs in this book have two major things in common—all were designed prior to World War II and all feature some degree of aerodynamic streamlining. Hungarian-born engineer Paul Jaray is credited as the father of automotive streamlining, having first improved the aerodynamics of Zeppelins and then applied the same principles of drag reduction to the automobile. The first car designed under his supervision, the Ley T6 of 1922, made such an impression that manufacturers large and small began producing their own teardrop-shaped prototypes and limited production cars, the most famous probably being the rear-engine Tatras of the 1930s. In addition to the scientifically streamlined cars of the interwar period, there were those that were streamlined for styling purposes—vehicles designed by John Tjaarda and Raymond Loewy, for instance, or the elegant and graceful designs of coachbuilders like Figoni et Falaschi. While they may not have had the low drag coefficients of the Jaray cars, they made up for it in sheer beauty and ostentation.

This book is obviously not a complete survey of streamlined automobiles of the interwar era; rather, it is a small survey of unrealized designs which have long intrigued me as an automotive enthusiast and illustrator. They range from relatively modest passenger cars to massive and powerful land speed record vehicles. The fact that only American and German automobiles are covered is largely accidental and should not be interpreted as a slight to other nations that contributed to the automotive streamlining movement, such as Czechoslovakia, France, Great Britain, Italy, and others. Perhaps projects from these countries can be covered in a future volume, assuming this one is successful.

In deciding on the subjects to cover, I focused on designs which had at least a fragmentary plan view; ideally, one would have a three-view with cross sections, but that wasn't the case with most of the automobiles featured herein. The majority of the 3D models are based on patent drawings which suffered from numerous inconsistencies, with the placement of key components shifting from view to view. The drawings inevitably lacked detail where they needed it, so I had to fill in the gaps concerning interiors, suspensions, tires, etc. from contemporary automobiles which were actually built. Not being an early 20th century automotive engineer, I have almost certainly made some questionable design decisions; in response to these inevitable criticisms, I can only plead artistic license. My intent was to add just enough detail to enhance the credibility of the artist's impressions without spoiling the designer's original intent; it was a tricky balancing act, as you can imagine.

Being based on patent drawings, most of the designs lacked dimensional data. I estimated the size of these vehicles using typical overall tire diameters of contemporary automobiles of a similar class. Hopefully these estimates will be of use to model companies wishing to create miniatures of these vehicles. Perhaps the book will inspire a wealthy automobile collector to commission a 1:1 recreation of one of these remarkable machines; I can certainly think of worse ways to spend your money.

The artwork is meant to be realistic but not hyper-realistic, as I did not have unlimited time to devote to this project. Some subjects were more difficult than others to model, texture and render; the unique challenges of illustrating each design are mentioned at the end of each chapter.

Concerning the name of each automobile, I used the original designation when known. However, for those designs derived from patents, a straightforward, economical name was often lacking. In these cases, I created a name based on the surname of the principal inventor and the patent description; these names are employed for sake of convenience and should not be considered definitive. The date of each design shown in the chapter heading is generally based on the filing date of the patent, if applicable.

I hope you enjoy seeing these fascinating and unorthodox vehicles brought to life through the magic of computer graphics; it took a lot of time and effort to put together, but I think the resulting book was worth it.

Jared A. Zichek
Hauser, Idaho
February 2017

CLARKE RACING VEHICLE

1916

This unusual automobile originates from US patent no. 1,214,897 for a radically streamlined racing vehicle designed by Harry D. Clarke of Omaha, Nebraska. The patent was assigned to the Efficiency Motor Corporation (possibly established by Clarke to produce the machine) and filed on July 3, 1916; the patent was awarded on February 6, 1917. Information about Clarke is lacking, though he also filed other patents for an automobile transmission, wheel hub, double-reduction drive, and other components during the 1919-20 period. He appears to have been an inventor with at least some formal engineering training, judging by the complexity of the items he patented.

According to the original document, the Clarke Racing Vehicle employed an internal combustion engine with a torpedo/cigar-shaped body to minimize the degree of air resistance when driven at high speed. The tapered front and rear ends resulted in a vehicle requiring less fuel and permitted a greater speed than usual. The body terminated at the rear with a cylindrical jacket containing the exhaust conduits, which were located at the vehicle's center line.

Another innovation was the provision of a chamber or compartment within the body midway between its ends for housing a driver and mechanic without appreciably increasing the size or diameter of the body, and to provide an aperture to enter the compartment and a transparent cover for the same which conformed to the general shape or contour of the body. This set it apart from typical race cars of the era, the majority of which featured drag-inducing upright windshields and open cabins.

The body circumscribed and extended below the vehicle frame to permit the seats for the occupants to be disposed below the frame and at an attitude below the driving shaft of the engine. This put the center of gravity lower than possible by any other construction, safeguarding the operators within the chamber from serious injury.

The most notable feature of the Clarke design was the installation of a pair of periscopes (described in the patent as a "plurality of mirrors") for reflecting rays of light to permit the occupants, or one of them, to visibly inspect

OPPOSITE: Artist's impressions of the radically streamlined Clarke Racing Vehicle of 1916. Forward vision was provided by a pair of periscopes projecting from the bodywork just in front of the cabin.

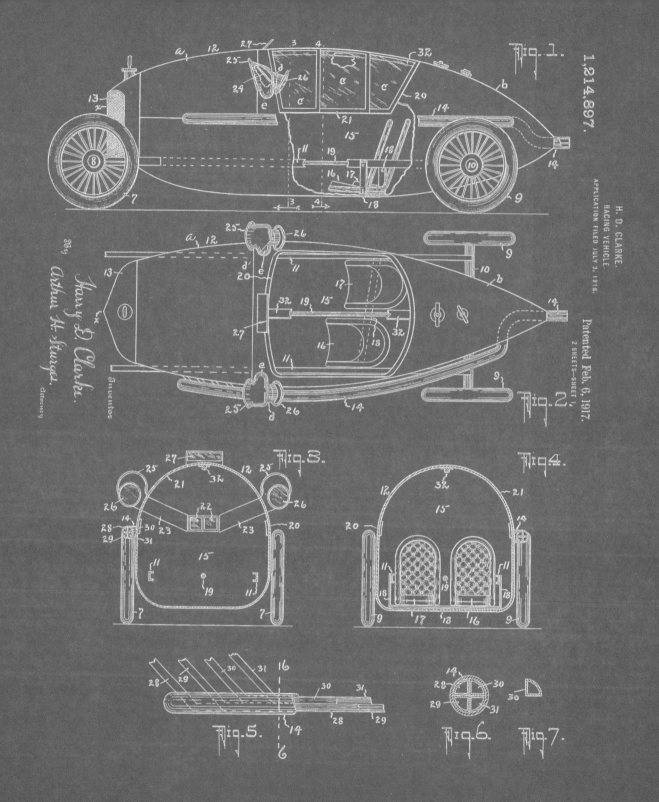

1,214,897.

H. D. CLARKE.
RACING VEHICLE.
APPLICATION FILED JULY 3, 1916.

Patented Feb. 6, 1917.
2 SHEETS—SHEET 1.

Fig.1.

Fig.2.

Fig.3.

Fig.4.

Fig.5.

Fig.6.

Fig.7.

Inventor
Harry D. Clarke.
By
Arthur A. Sturges.
Attorney

the roadway at both front and rear, and for an examination of the front and rear wheels of the vehicle.

The patent mentioned that changes in form, size, proportion and minor details could be made to the design, as determined by the scope of the appended claims. Thus, the configuration shown in the patent may have differed somewhat from the actual vehicle, had it ever left the drawing board.

Since the vehicle was designed for racing and for driving on good roads, the body could have been sealed to exclude dust and in-rushing air, and its lower side or bottom disposed very near or close to the ground while circumscribing the frame, its top preferably being disposed at a sufficient height to suitably enclose the engine.

Within the driving compartment, the seats were disposed in a plane below the frame, adjacent to the lower wall of the body and, preferably, being connected to the saddle or strip which was substantially of a U-shape and secured at its upper ends to the frame. The driver and mechanic were seated at the respective sides of the driving shaft of the engine, entirely within and housed by the body envelope, with no objectionable pockets or recesses on the outside which would materially interfere with the operation. The cabin was completely covered with a suitable frame and curved glass panels which conformed to the convex form or contour of the body.

During operation of the Clarke Racing Vehicle, on account of the position occupied by the driver and mechanic, objects on the roadway at the front and rear of the vehicle would not ordinarily be visible to them, and therefore a pair of angled periscopes were provided, with the inclination of the mirrors being such that the front wheels, the roadway in front of the vehicle, or objects on the roadway could be conveniently and readily seen by the driver and mechanic during operation.

From a modern perspective, the periscope installation appears problematic. First, the driver was provided with a small set of mirrors within the vehicle for forward vision, affording him much less visibility than in a race car of conventional configuration. This would have made driving the machine more hazardous than its contemporaries. Forward visibility would have been further degraded by the outer glass of the periscopes becoming obscured by rain, grime, dust, etc.

The outer parts of the periscopes, which gave the vehicle a frog-eyed appearance when viewed from the front, would have created significant drag, at least partially offsetting the improvement in speed afforded by the aerodynamic body and enclosed cabin. The projecting parts of the periscopes could have been better designed, with transparent aerodynamic fairings in front to reduce air resistance, for example.

A pair of mirrors were mounted on the backs of the periscopes, allowing the driver and mechanic to view the rear wheels and the roadway at the rear of the vehicle. These were supplemented by a single, inclined rear view mirror located on top of the vehicle in front of the transparent enclosure.

The exhaust port of each engine cylinder

OPPOSITE: Original patent drawings of the Clarke Racing Vehicle.

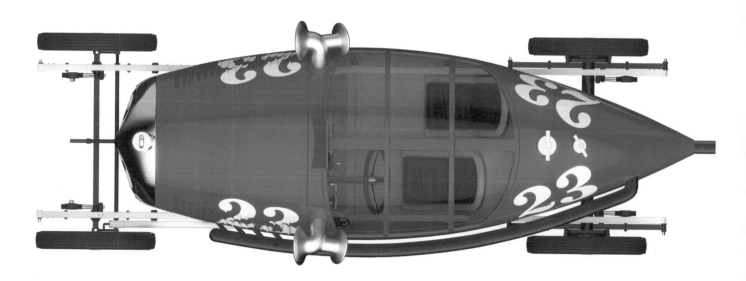

Note: I estimated the dimensions based on an overall tire diameter of 34 inches (864 mm)—a typical size for the period. Actual size of the vehicle is unknown.

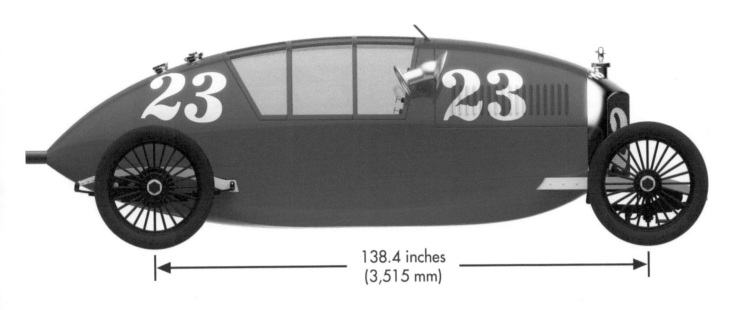

138.4 inches
(3,515 mm)

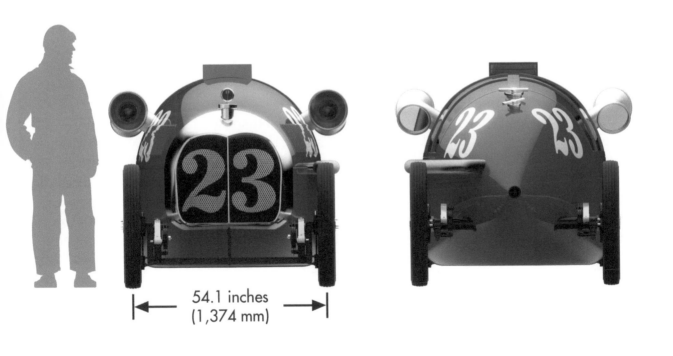

54.1 inches
(1,374 mm)

was provided with a separate conduit to channel the gases to the atmosphere. A four cylinder engine was envisaged for the design, with each of the four exhaust conduits being of segmental form in cross section. The exhaust pipe had a longitudinal curvature conforming to the wall and disposed on the left side of the body.

This arrangement permitted the exhaust conduits to discharge to the atmosphere in line with the longitudinal axis of the vehicle, with the force derived from these discharges potentially increasing the maximum speed of the racing vehicle.

According to Clarke, his automobile design practically eliminated the danger ordinarily associated with the driving of such machines, with the center of gravity being located much lower than was possible with conventional construction, thereby tending to prevent rollovers. A curved truss bar conforming to the shape of the body and disposed in the medial line, at the upper part thereof, below the cover, provided a firm structural support for the cover, reinforced the body, and operated as a shield to protect the driver and mechanic, if the vehicle overturned.

Clarke believed that the chance of injury to the occupants of the race car was reduced to a minimum. The aerodynamic form of the body, along with other features mentioned, enabled the vehicle to attain a very high degree of speed, depending only upon the character of the engine employed. The wedge-shaped radiator also

TOP: Aft view of the vehicle showing the mirror installation, with one mounted on the back of each periscope housing and a narrow rectangular mirror located on the centerline forward of the passenger compartment.

A rear elevated view of the driver's compartment showing the very small periscope mirrors provided for forward vision. The instrumentation and internal details are speculative, being based on various race cars of the era, such as Duesenbergs.

helped to reduce air resistance when the vehicle was at speed.

With over a century of hindsight, it seems doubtful that a driver and mechanic would have risked their lives driving this car in competition; the forward field of view would have been especially poor, contrary to Clarke's claims, and excellent visibility is critical in racing. Prospective drivers probably would have regarded the vehicle as a rolling death trap, with the interior likely being intolerably hot and confined, especially in the event of an accident, where the ability to make a quick exit was critical to survival. With some modification to the periscopes, the configuration of the Clarke Racing Vehicle was better suited to land speed record attempts at the Bonneville Salt Flats than competitive racing.

Investors were likely also skeptical of the periscope system, which may have been the primary reason the Clarke Racing Vehicle was never built. In addition, Omaha, Nebraska was not the nexus of American automotive development, making the accumulation of necessary capital, components and expertise to build it more challenging. The other innovations of the design, such as the streamlining, low center of gravity, and exhaust arrangement had some merit, but were not enough to make the machine a reality.

Notes on the Artist's Impressions

This was one of the most time-consuming cars in the book to illustrate due to the exposed suspension and lack of detail in the original patent drawings. To make the artist's impressions more credible, I added axles, leaf springs, shock absorbers, brakes, and other components to the design; these were based on contemporary American race cars, primarily Duesenbergs. I extended the frame rails both fore and aft to accommodate the leaf springs and other components.

Except for those items shown in the patent drawings, details of the interior are also speculative and based on contemporary race cars. The outer rear portion of the periscope casings were quite difficult to translate into 3D; these were simplified into something that made more sense from a design standpoint. The design of the wheels was unusual, somewhere between the artillery wheels of early Bearcat racers and the wire wheels that came later in the decade. I added louvers to the hood for cooling purposes. The color schemes are inspired by surviving American race cars of the period.

The patent provides no information on the actual size of the vehicle, which is not uncommon in these documents. In estimating the dimensions of the racer, I assumed it had an overall tire diameter of 34 inches (854 mm), which was typical of several race cars in this period. This resulted in a vehicle with a wheelbase of 138.4 inches (3,515 mm) and a track of 54.1 inches (1,374 mm), making it a relatively large if low-slung racer, as shown in the orthographic views on pages 10–11. For reference, the driver silhouettes included in the orthographic views throughout the book are scaled at 6 ft (1.83 m) tall.

This front bird's eye view of the Clarke Racing Vehicle emphasizes the extraordinary (if somewhat impractical) cleanliness of the design, especially compared to contemporary grand prix racers of the early twentieth century.

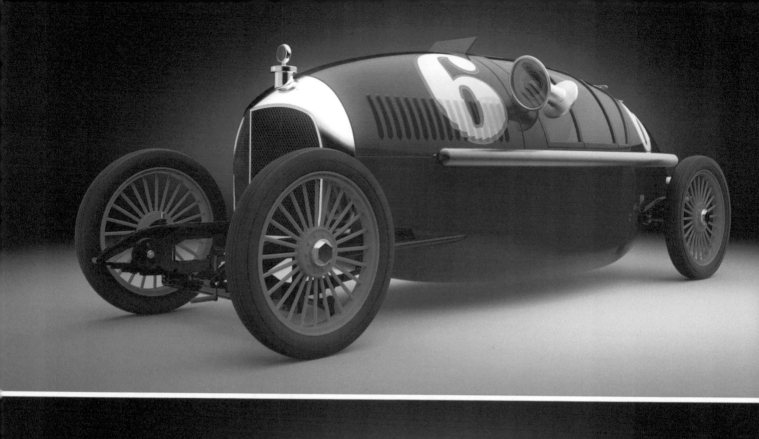

TOP: The Clarke Racing Vehicle in an alternate color scheme inspired by a restored Miller race car of the early 1920s.

OPPOSITE: Two additional color schemes based on surviving American race cars of the teens and twenties. Regardless of the livery, the Clarke design remains both striking and bizarre, even by modern standards.

HENNINGER POWER DRIVEN VEHICLE

1924

This singular streamliner is based on US patent no. 1,523,263 filed April 5, 1924 by Albert Berthold Henninger of Berlin-Wilmersdorf, Germany; the patent was awarded on January 13, 1925. Henninger is a rather obscure figure in German automotive history with little information available concerning his background; this doesn't diminish the ideas presented in his patent, however, which related to motor driven vehicles of all kinds both for railways and roads. The object of the invention was to produce a vehicle with the lowest possible drag. This was accomplished by giving the body of the vehicle the shape of "half the surface generated by the rotation of a streamline corresponding substantially to that of an elongated drop of fluid;" i.e., half a teardrop. The sides of the body were somewhat depressed so as to make it better adapted for the occupants. The body was provided with a bottom that was flat at its widest portion but was curved near the end of the main portion of the body, the curvature increasing towards the end. The edges at which the body was connected to the bottom of the vehicle were also rounded in accordance with the invention.

A further feature of the Henninger de-sign consisted in covering the other parts of the vehicle which were not situated within the main portion of the vehicle body in streamlined fairings. Thus, two thirds of each wheel was enclosed in such a fairing. This also applied to the axle that connected the front pair of wheels and was outside the main portion of the vehicle body. The steps and connecting portions which joined the wheel fairings with the main portion of the vehicle body were also of streamlined form.

The streamlined wheel fairings were arranged so as to partly move and also turn laterally with the wheels. The parts of the fairings that turned with the wheels could be arranged to carry the headlights, these lights also being housed in streamlined fairings. By thus arranging the headlights to turn with the wheels, the light was always thrown in the direction in which the wheels were turned. These headlights were supplemented by a single large central light located in the front of the main body of the

---

OPPOSITE: The basic shape of the Henninger Power Driven Vehicle of 1924 was based on a bisected teardrop with flattened sides, supplemented by additional streamlined fairings covering the wheels, front axle, etc.

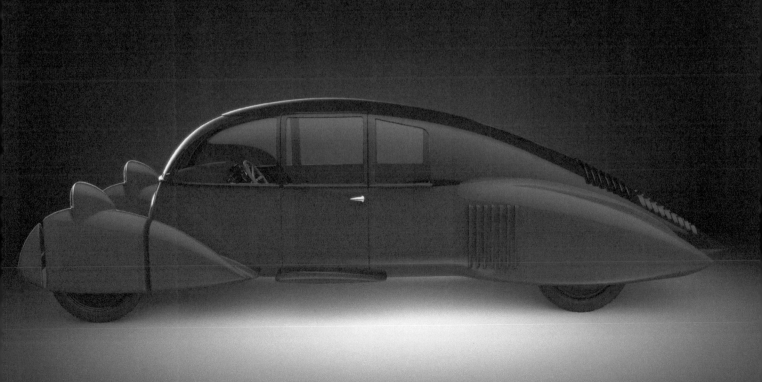

A. B. HENNINGER

POWER DRIVEN VEHICLE

Filed April 5. 1924

Fig. 1.

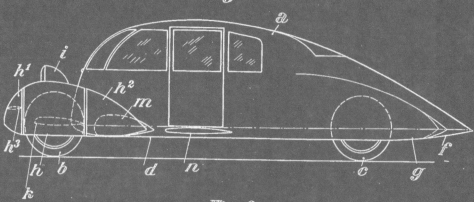

Fig. 2.

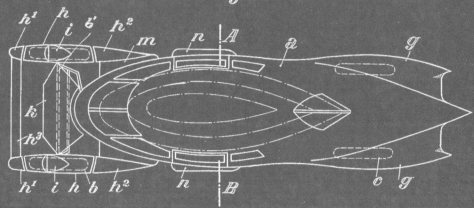

Fig. 3.

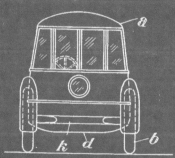

Fig. 4.

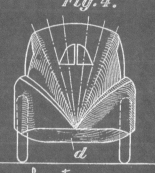

Inventor
Albert Berthold Henninger
by Knight Bro attorneys.

vehicle.

The wheels could be advantageously arranged entirely or partly in the main portion of the streamlined vehicle body or they could be entirely or partly placed in projecting portions attached to the main body.

The outline of the main body of the vehicle as viewed from the side and above had a streamlined shape. The entire portion above the dash and dot line in *Figure 1* of the patent had the form of half a teardrop. The bottom of the main portion was parallel to the ground except at the front and rear where it curved upwards. The bottom surface of the main portion of the vehicle body, that is the part beneath the dash and dot line, was flat up to the point where the cross section was largest, that is up to the plane *A-B* in *Figure 2*, and at the rear it was curved, the curvature of the vehicle increasing transversely towards the end. The main portion of the vehicle body had the form of a teardrop but its sides were slightly depressed. Radial sections taken along the dash and dot lines indicated in *Figure 4* all had the form of half a teardrop. The rear wheels were partly arranged in projections or fins connected to the main portion of the vehicle body. The front wheels were arranged in fairings, in the front and rear of which were separate small fairings. These three fairings taken together formed a streamlined body, preferably a teardrop, but with considerably depressed sides. The middle portion was arranged to turn with the wheels. Placed upon the middle portion of each wheel fairing was a streamlined form housing a headlight.

OPPOSITE: Original patent drawings of the Henninger Power Driven Vehicle filed April 5, 1924.

The front sections of the fairings that enveloped the wheels were interconnected by a cross piece which was of streamlined form. The front axle was also enclosed in an aerodynamic fairing, this fairing being beveled at the sides so as to enable the wheels to be turned for the purpose of steering the vehicle. The cross piece could have been connected to the main body of the vehicle in any desired way, such as by suitable supports (not shown in the patent) extending from the fairing covering the front axle.

The fairings behind the front wheels were connected to the main body by a connecting piece also of streamlined form. Drag reduction was also applied to the entry steps. About two thirds of the wheels were enclosed in fairings or in the main body of the vehicle.

Henninger's design may have been influenced by the Rumpler *Tropfenwagen* (Teardrop Car), an early streamlined vehicle produced from 1921-1925 in Berlin-Johannisthal, Germany. No great success, most of the vehicles ended up being sold as taxis in the Berlin area; Henninger, a Berlin resident, probably encountered them on a regular basis. Both cars share a cyclopean central headlight as a design feature and both were heavily streamlined, though to different degrees. Henninger's design could be looked at as an improved Tropfenwagen, with greater attention paid to streamlining the top of the vehicle and enclosing the wheels in streamlined fairings.

The commercial failure of the Rumpler Tropfenwagen, only about 100 of which were produced, may be part of the reason that Henninger's vehicle remained a stillborn design. Potential financial backers likely realized that

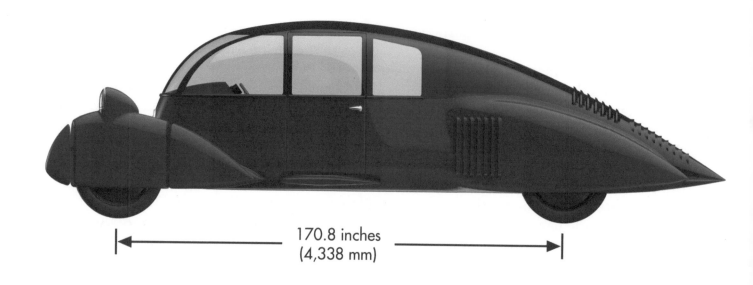

170.8 inches
(4,338 mm)

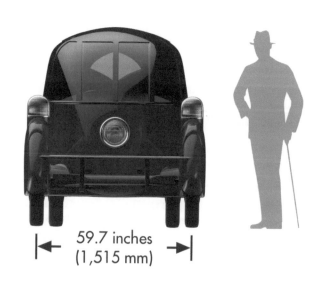

59.7 inches
(1,515 mm)

Note: I estimated the dimensions based on an overall tire diameter of 34.65 inches (880 mm)—the same as the Rumpler Tropfenwagen. Actual size of the car is unknown.

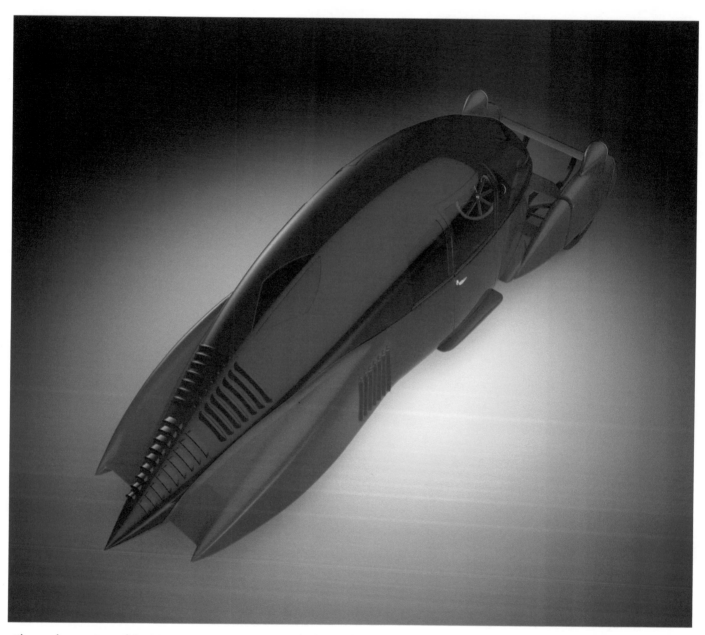

Elevated rear view of the Henninger Power Driven Vehicle emphasizing its long, narrow body and boat tail styling. Speculative louvers have been added to provide ventilation for the engine; these are inspired by the Rumpler Tropfenwagen.

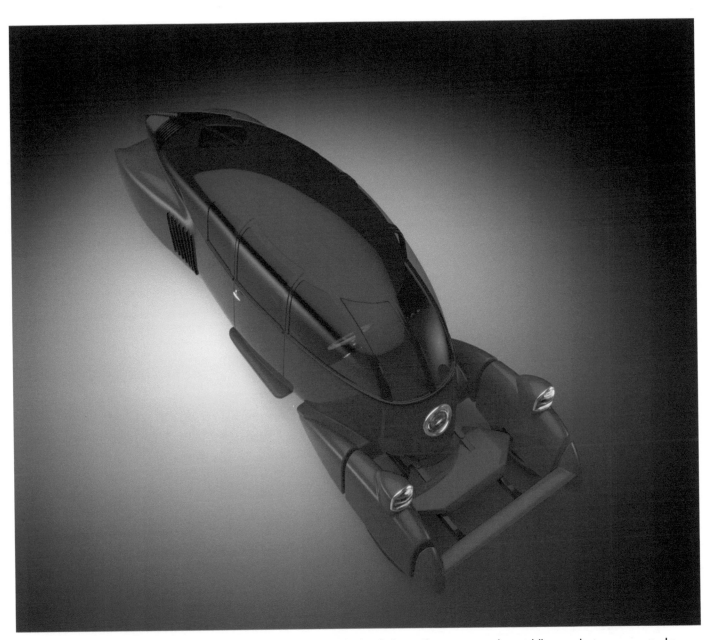

The streamlined fairings covering the front wheels were each divided into three pieces, the middle part being separated to permit turning. Frame rails were added extending from the main body to support the axle and front cross piece, as these components were basically floating in space in the original patent drawings.

the public had rejected the Tropfenwagen and probably would do the same with Henninger's car, which was even more radically streamlined and unorthodox. Henninger's obscurity suggests that he did not have ties to a large company, which made getting his vehicle produced more difficult. The fragile economic situation in Germany, which had just gone through hyperinflation when Henninger's patent was filed, was also a possible factor contributing to the car's failure to reach the hardware stage.

TOP: Rear view of Henninger's streamlined automobile. Drag reduction was paramount, with even the entry steps being optimized to reduce air resistance.

OPPOSITE: Alternate color schemes inspired by the Rumpler Tropfenwagen, which may have influenced the design of Henninger's car.

Notes on the Artist's Impressions

Lacking information on the vehicle's actual size, I assumed that it had the same overall tire diameter as the Rumpler Tropfenwagen, which was 34.65 inches (880 mm). This resulted in a wheelbase of 170.8 inches (4,338 mm) and a front wheel track of 59.7 inches (1,515 mm). I guessed that Henninger's design was a mid-engine vehicle like the Tropfenwagen, adding louvers along the rear sides and on top of the boat tail. I also added frame rails to support the front axle and the crosspiece that connected the two fairings forward of the front wheels; leaf springs were incorporated as well. The color schemes are inspired by those possibly worn by the Tropfenwagen.

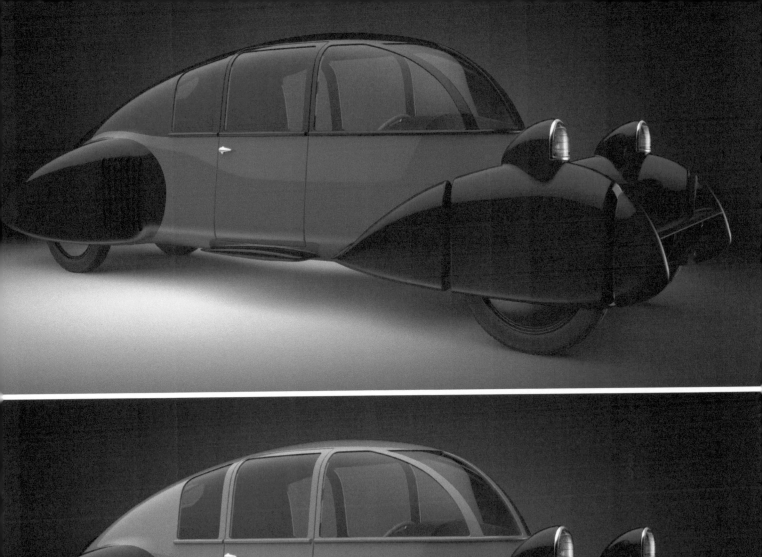
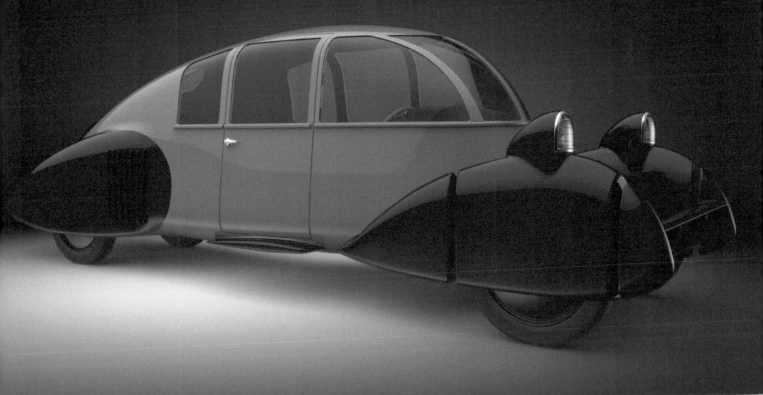

The resulting vehicle is not what I'd call a beautiful automobile—it's somewhat reminiscent of a lobster on wheels—but the Henninger Power Driven Vehicle was certainly innovative, especially compared to the upright styling of typical automobiles of the 1920s.

TOP: The Henninger Power Driven Vehicle in another speculative color scheme inspired by the Tropfenwagen.

RYSTEDT MOTOR CAR

1925

The car featured in this chapter originates from an American patent filed on April 22, 1925 by Ingemar K. Rystedt; one-half of the patent was assigned to Chester R. Snyder, both of Dayton, Ohio. Rystedt was an automotive and aircraft inventor who previously helped found the Wizard Spark Plug Co. in Dayton in 1919. Snyder may have been a financial backer of the project, though this is pure speculation.

According to the patent, the Rystedt Motor Car was a passenger automobile of a design and construction which was a radical departure from conventional motor vehicles. It was a fully streamlined design optimized to reduce head air pressure and to balance the air pressure on the top and underside of the car. The vehicle is reminiscent of the Castagna Alfa Romeo 40/60 HP *Aerodinamica* of 1914, though somewhat more refined in appearance, resembling a dirigible on wheels.

An additional departure from common practice was the installation of pneumatic shock absorbing elements to the chassis of the machine, as opposed to the springs and various types of mechanical shock absorbers used by contemporary autos. The motor was enclosed within the main body portion to effect a fully streamlined construction and to gain the further advantage of heating the interior of the car in cold weather directly from the motor, adjustable windows being provided to afford ample ventilation in milder seasons.

All projections were eliminated, such as fenders, foot boards, head lights, tire carriers, and so forth, all such equipment of the car being contained within the lateral body lines. This provided protection for these items, which were often damaged on more conventional automobiles; it also reduced overall drag.

Rystedt believed that his design anticipated a general trend towards the streamlining of automobiles in the future. The features shown in his patent only served to illustrate the novel principles upon which an improved car could be constructed, with the understanding that suitable modifications were contemplated to make the vehicle commercially viable. Thus, the design shown in the patent was not finalized and a production version would have likely featured numerous modifications.

The shock absorbing elements consisted of pneumatic bags or cushions adapted to be inflated by means of a valve; the pressure

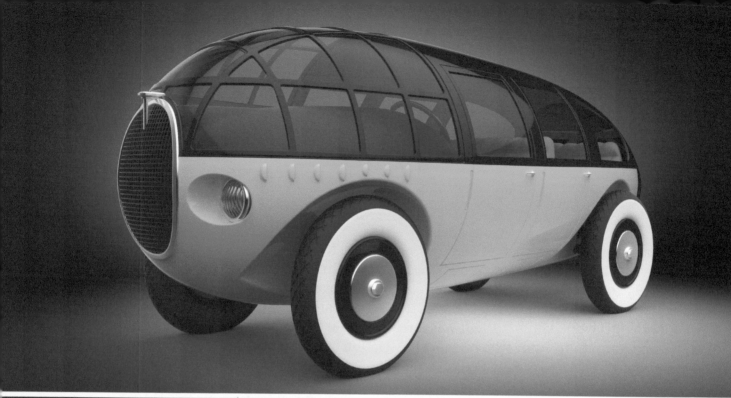

would have been regulated according to the load carried. Rystedt anticipated quiet, easy riding conditions of the motor car resulting from shock-absorbing elements interposed between the front and rear axles and the complete elimination of springs made possible by this arrangement.

Pneumatic suspension was first introduced in 1909 by the Cowey Motor Works of Great Britain, but it was unreliable and failed to catch on. The experimental Stout-Scarab of 1933 incorporated the first practical pneumatic suspension, which was developed by Firestone. Interestingly, the Stout-Scarab shared a similar design philosophy to the Rystedt Motor Car and has become a classic example of streamlined automotive design.

The body of the Rystedt car was described as a having a "turtle-back" shell with four doors, each having a foldable step which deployed when the door was opened and retracted flush with the body when closed. Both the front and rear wheels were within the body lines, the body being undercut to provide clearance for the front wheels required for steering, fenders and footboards being entirely eliminated. The head lights and radiator were designed to reduce parasitic drag, and a glass enclosed "observation deck" was provided at the front of the machine to afford ample visibility and to admit light to the interior, with the front panel being made adjustable for ventilation. The doors and rear portion of the body were provided with glass panels.

A compartment for spare tires was located at the rear of the machine and closed by a door or removable panel along the side. A smaller compartment for luggage by lid or cover was placed aft of the rearmost window.

In the patent, Rystedt also described a modified construction of the chassis frame, with the lower frame member being used in conjunction with the frame and a buffer or shock absorber comprising oppositely acting compression springs supported in upper and lower brackets and secured to the chassis frames. This was to compensate for the end thrust of the frames and to minimize sudden shocks to the machine, thus further improving its riding qualities.

From the perspective of an automotive enthusiast, it is unfortunate that not even a prototype Rystedt Motor Car was built and preserved, as it is a rather appealing example of early streamlining. However, it is unlikely that the vehicle would have been a success, given the public reception of other early American streamliners, such as the Dymaxion (1933), Stout-Scarab (1932-46), and the greatest commercial failure of all, the Chrysler Airflow (1934-37). If the American public of the 1930s wasn't ready for radically streamlined automobiles, then the public of the 1920s was probably even less so.

One could imagine a scenario where a prototype Rystedt Motor Car was built and received widespread publicity, possibly accelerating broader acceptance of these types of vehicles, giving later cars like the Airflow a better chance of success. The relative obscurity

I. K. RYSTEDT

MOTOR CAR

Filed April 22, 1925

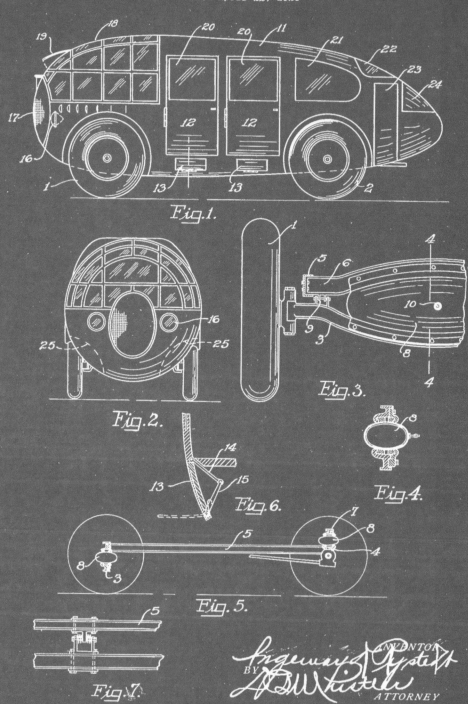

Fig.1.

Fig.2.

Fig.3.

Fig.6.

Fig.4.

Fig.5.

Fig.7.

INVENTOR
Ingemar K. Rystedt
BY
ATTORNEY

of Ingemar K. Rystedt suggests that he lacked the business connections and acumen to make his design a reality, a common problem among independent designers outside of a major company.

Notes on the Artist's Impressions

In addition to the patent, an original artist's rendering of this car by C.C. Bratten survives; it is titled "Design for a Streamline Motor Car by Ingemar K. Rystedt" and dates from 1925.[1] The profile of the vehicle is noticeably exaggerated to make it look longer and sleeker than the design shown in the patent drawings, a common practice in automotive marketing artwork. This vintage illustration influenced my choice of color scheme, placement of interior details, and helped make sense of the patent drawings, where there was especially poor agreement between the side and front elevations. For example, the radiator was higher in the front view than the side and the frame of the greenhouse windshield did not match; I relied mostly on the side view in modeling the vehicle. I also found that I had to inset the headlights to approximate the location shown in the drawings. The front view shows an abrupt transition from a circular cross section at the aft edge of

TOP: Rear view of the Rystedt Motor Car emphasizing its tapered rear end. The aft vertical doors on the tail provided access to spare tires, while the small rear upper compartment served as the trunk

OPPOSITE: Patent drawings of the Rystedt Motor Car dating from 1925.

33

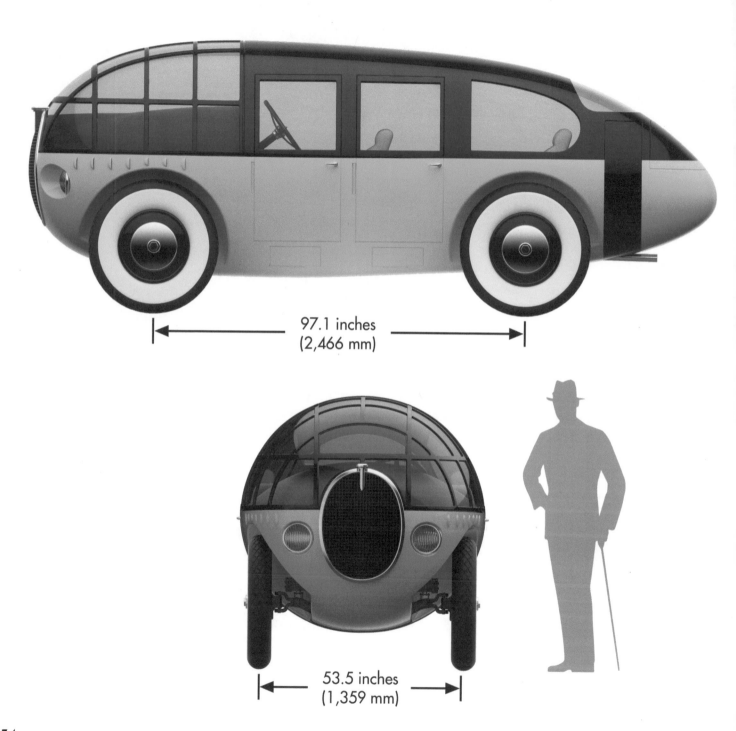

97.1 inches
(2,466 mm)

53.5 inches
(1,359 mm)

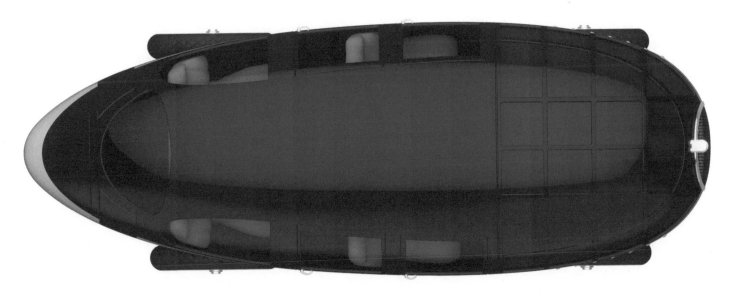

Note: I estimated the dimensions based on an overall tire diameter of 34 inches (864 mm)—a typical size for this type of vehicle in the 1920s. Actual size of the car is unknown.

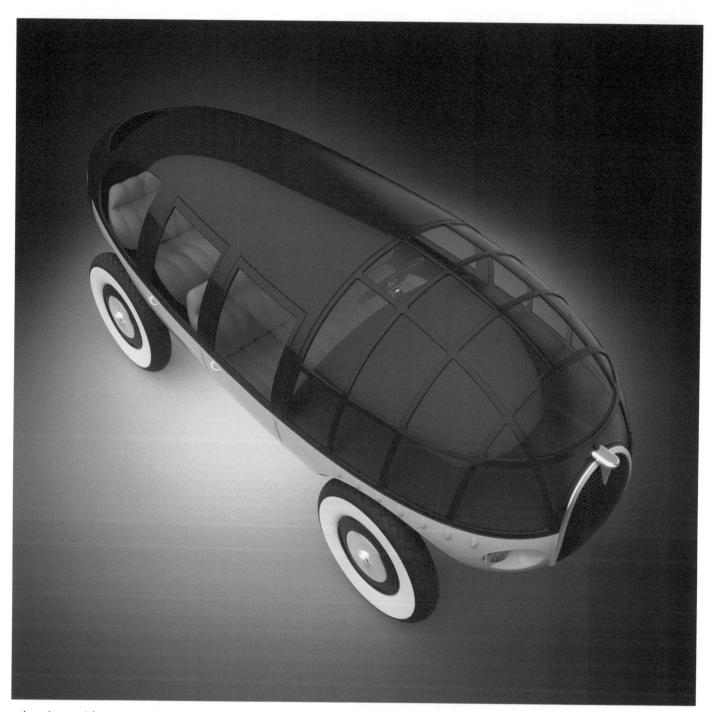

This elevated front view of the vehicle highlights the enormous dash necessitated by the large greenhouse windshield and front engine placement; it is based on C.C. Bratten's vintage artwork of the car, which shows details not in the patent.

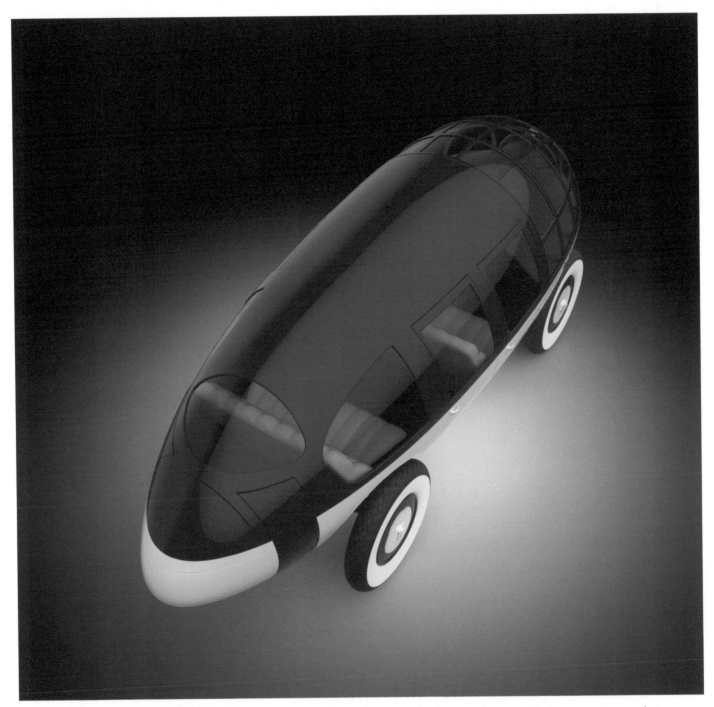

Rear bird's eye view of Rystedt's concept, which resembled a blimp on wheels. Seat design and placement is speculative.

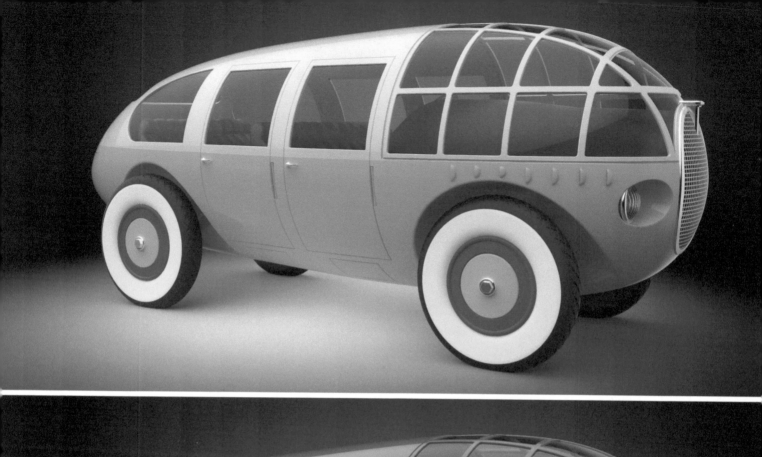
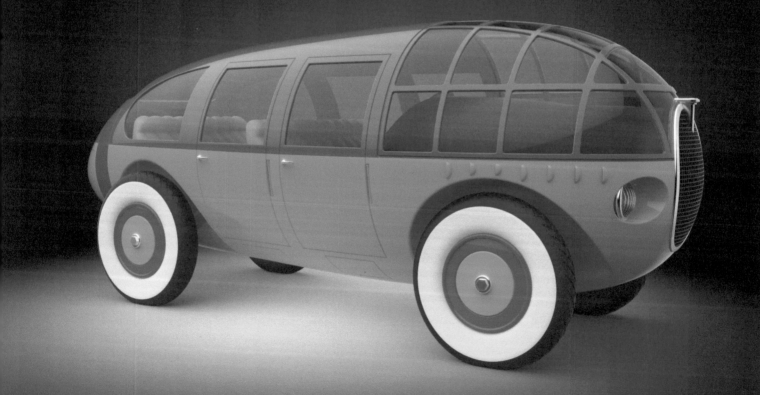

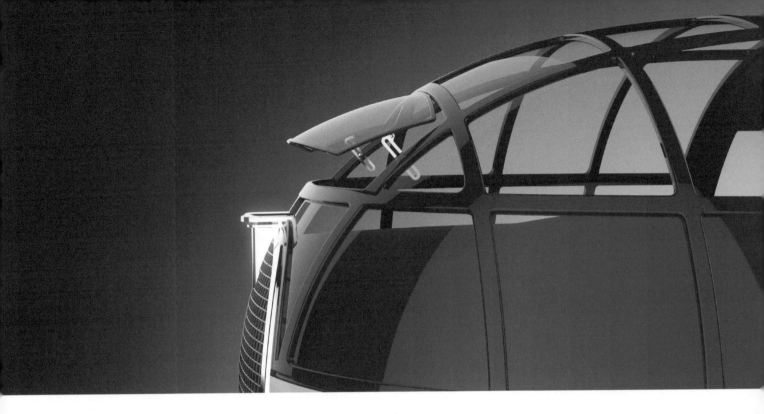

the windshield to a boxier cross section in the passenger area; when modeled in 3D, the result appeared rather awkward, so I decided to maintain a basically circular cross section throughout, as implied by the Bratten illustration. If a clay model of this design had been done, I think the cross sections would have been modified to make the lines of the vehicle flow better than indicated in the patent.

TOP: Closeup of the forward window which opened to provide ventilation for the passenger compartment; hinge details are speculative.

OPPOSITE: Some color variations of the Rystedt Motor Car inspired by restored American classics of the 1920s.

VALIER-LIPPISCH WINGED VEHICLES

1928

These unusual designs were the result of a collaboration between two famous Germanic technical pioneers: Max Valier and Alexander Lippisch. Valier was an Austrian rocketry advocate known for developing a number of spectacular rocket-powered vehicles in partnership with Fritz von Opel in the 1920s. Lippisch was a German aeronautical engineer who made great contributions to the development of tailless aircraft and the delta wing, his most famous design being the Messerschmitt Me 163 rocket-powered interceptor of World War II. The result of the Valier-Lippisch partnership can be found in German patent no. 499,199 dated June 7, 1928, titled *Kraftwagen für hohe Fahrgeschwindigkeit mit zu beiden Seiten des Fahrzeuges angeordneten Tragflächenansätzen*. This can be translated as "High Speed Motor Vehicle with Wing Assemblies Arranged on Both Sides of the Vehicle."

According to the patent, for high speed automobiles of any propulsion, especially a rocket-propelled race car, the vehicle's body required a total or partially streamlined form to reduce air resistance. The addition of downforce generating wings could help overcome the completely inadequate tire grip of contemporary automobiles, especially those of lighter weight. However, experiments with automobiles equipped with such devices (such as the Opel RAK.2 of 1928) had resulted in intermittent disturbances of the airflow at high speed, causing the driver to lose control of the vehicle. In order to safely achieve very high speeds, a new automobile shape was required which generated sufficient downforce to ensure good contact with the road and improve driving controllability.

With this invention, the attachment of wings or wing assemblies, alone or in combination with the automobile body, constituted an aerodynamically stable system which created longitudinal stability, while the addition of vertical surfaces or surface assemblies provided

OPPOSITE: Artist's impressions of the Valier-Lippisch Vehicle 1 of 1928. This unusual rocket-propelled machine featured aerodynamic surfaces placed fore aft to improve overall stability at high speeds.

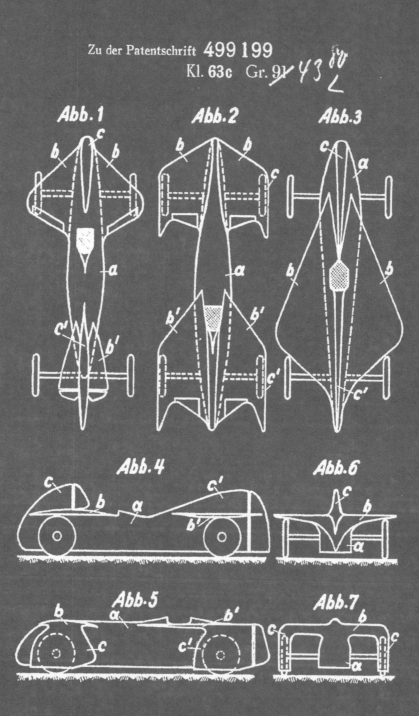

lateral stability. The failure of previous vehicles was attributable to the fact that a streamlined body with a lateral discharge of air produced a total aerodynamic force where the center or pressure was located at or in front of the tip of the streamlined form. An increase in the automobile nose area reduced the downforce effect of the wing assemblies, converting the airflow into lift. In the first case, a side wind gust would push the automobile off course from the center line by lateral pressure. In the second case, a pitch up of the nose or even the vehicle becoming airborne could occur.

The patent illustrated three possible configurations of wing-equipped automobile. *Abbildung* (Figure) 1 shows a conventional aircraft type, Abbildung 2 is a canard (tail first), and Abbildung 3 is a tailless aircraft type; for sake of convenience, I will refer to these as Vehicles 1, 2 and 3, respectively.

Vehicles 1 and 2 featured a streamlined body with wing stubs attached fore and aft, the size and cross-section of which were so arranged as to produce partial aerodynamic forces with strong forward acceleration, resulting in a total force moving through the center of gravity which also dampened longitudinal oscillations. In these vehicles, the front pair of wings always bore the higher specific aerodynamic pressure load. Vehicle 3 featured a single arrow-shaped and inherently stable wing, specifically the delta wing for which Lippisch would later become famous.

All three vehicles had various vertical surface arrangements to provide lateral stabili-

ty. Vehicle 1 was equipped with vertical surfaces on the longitudinal axis fore and aft of the center of gravity. In a similar way to the horizontal surfaces, the lateral deflection of the vertical fins produced a total force moving through the vertical center of gravity.

In the case of Vehicle 2, the vertical surfaces also served as streamlined wheel coverings to reduce the drag of the wheels.

In each configuration, the vertical surfaces were rigidly connected to the body of the vehicle. However, they could have also been designed to be completely or partially adjusted by the driver, similar to aircraft control surfaces. This adjustment could have been coupled with or independent of the steering, according to the requirement.

Depending upon the requirement, any combination of vertical and horizontal surfaces shown in the patent was possible; to keep things simple, only the configurations actually shown in Abbildungen 1-7 have been illustrated.

At the time the patent was filed, Lippisch had been designing a series of unconventional gliders, including canard and tailless types; despite their high performance, these designs were attracting little interest from the government or private industry. The automotive industry, being perhaps even more conservative than their aviation counterpart, made no rush to adapt the ideas presented in the Valier-Lippisch patent.

Valier lost an important patron when Fritz von Opel left his family firm after 1929. He briefly found a new one with Paul Heylandt, but the Heylandt company was smaller than Opel and could not offer the same financial support. The Valier-Heylandt Rak. 7, first tested by

---

OPPOSITE: Original patent drawings of the Valier-Lippisch Winged Vehicles dating from 1928.

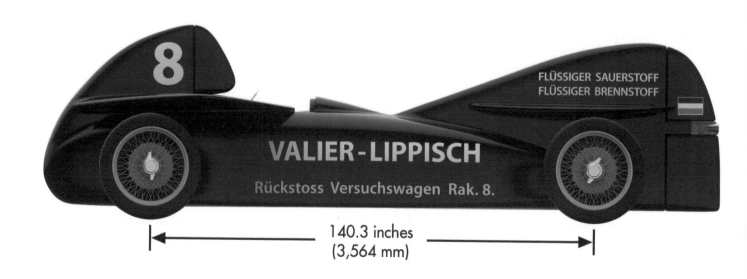

8

FLÜSSIGER SAUERSTOFF
FLÜSSIGER BRENNSTOFF

VALIER-LIPPISCH

Rückstoss Versuchswagen Rak. 8.

140.3 inches
(3,564 mm)

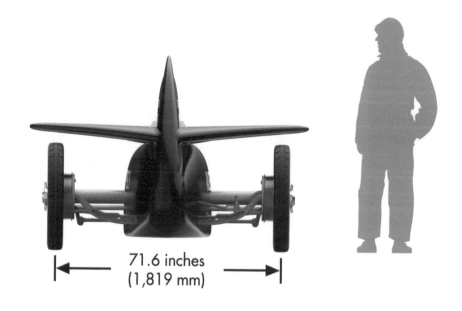

71.6 inches
(1,819 mm)

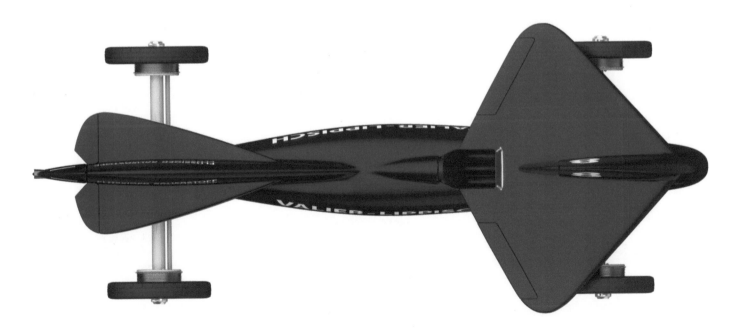

Note: I estimated the dimensions based on an overall tire diameter of 32.28 inches (820 mm)—the same size of tire used on a reproduction of the Opel RAK.2. Actual size of the design is unknown.

This elevated front view highlights the poor forward vision permitted by the front wing and fin. Racing the vehicle competitively likely would have been out of the question, but speed record attempts were certainly possible.

The layout of Vehicle 1's aerodynamic surfaces was based on that of a conventional aircraft, with a supplemental vertical fin and rudder placed at the front for additional lateral stability at high speeds.

On the car: **8** · VALIER-LIPPISCH · Rückstoss Versuchswagen Rak · FLÜSSIGER SAUERSTOFF FLÜSSIGER BRENNSTOFF

Valier on April 19, 1930, was a rather primitive vehicle compared to the Opel RAK.2 of 1928, except for the rocket engine. Heylandt probably was unwilling or unable to invest the necessary capital to realize one of the winged Valier-Lippisch concepts, which likely required significant wind tunnel work to properly develop.

Valier was accidentally killed May 17, 1930 when an alcohol-fueled rocket exploded on his test bench in Berlin. The death of Valier

probably destroyed the chances of one of these designs ever leaving the drawing board, as Lippisch was thoroughly focused on aeronautics and not the promoter that Valier was. The Pietsch-Heylandt rocket car of 1931 built upon Valier's earlier work, featuring a much improved liquid rocket engine, but did not incorporate the aerodynamic innovations of the Valier-Lippisch patent.

The Valier-Lippisch designs were ahead of their time, with downforce-generating wings being essential features of modern F1 cars. While the placement and arrangement of the wings on these early concepts appear rather odd to modern eyes, the essential principle of using aerodynamic surfaces to create downforce and improve overall stability at high speeds was sound.

TOP: I split the rudder into two pieces to accommodate the rocket nozzle at the rear of the vehicle. The design and location of the nozzle is based on the Pietsch-Heylandt rocket car of 1931.

OPPOSITE: Valier-Lippisch Vehicle 2 featured streamlined wheel coverings to reduce drag and improve the lateral stability of the vehicle at high speeds.

ALIER-LIPPISCH
oss Versuchswagen Rak. 8.
8
FLÜSSIGER SAUERSTOFF
FLÜSSIGER BRENNSTOFF

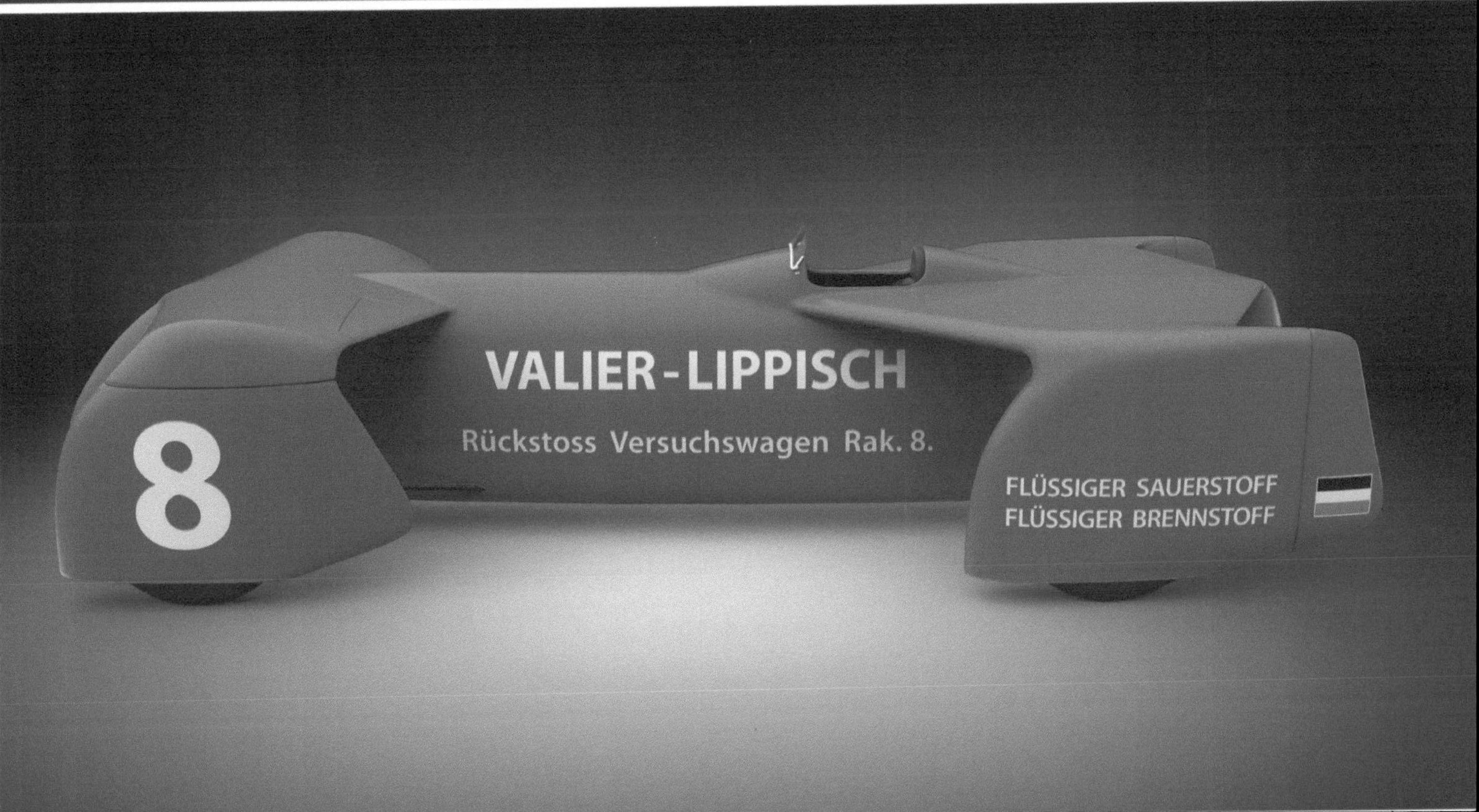
VALIER-LIPPISCH
Rückstoss Versuchswagen Rak. 8.
8
FLÜSSIGER SAUERSTOFF
FLÜSSIGER BRENNSTOFF

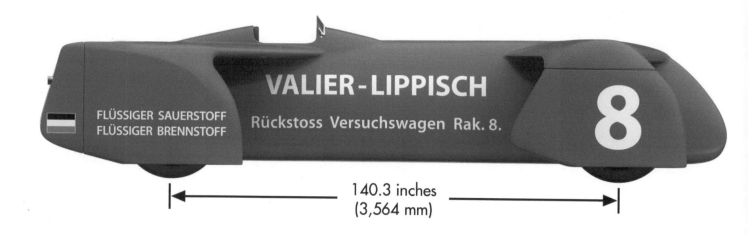

VALIER-LIPPISCH

FLÜSSIGER SAUERSTOFF
FLÜSSIGER BRENNSTOFF

Rückstoss Versuchswagen Rak. 8.

8

140.3 inches
(3,564 mm)

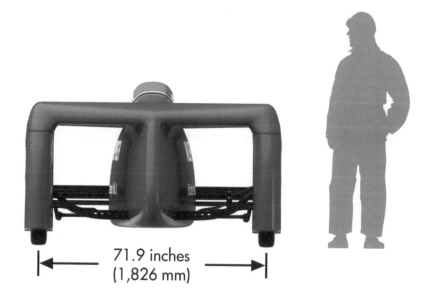

71.9 inches
(1,826 mm)

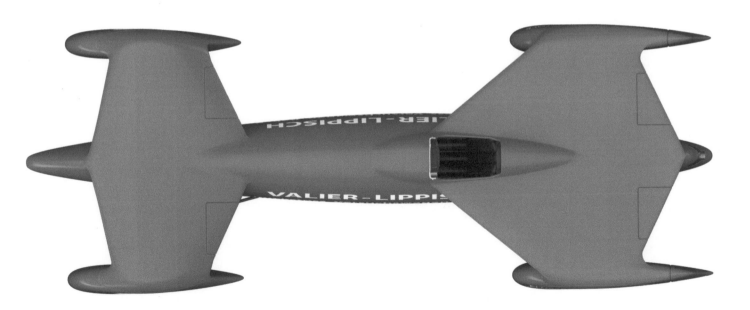

Note: I estimated the dimensions based on an overall tire diameter of 32.28 inches (820 mm)—the same size of tire used on a reproduction of the Opel RAK.2. Actual size of the design is unknown.

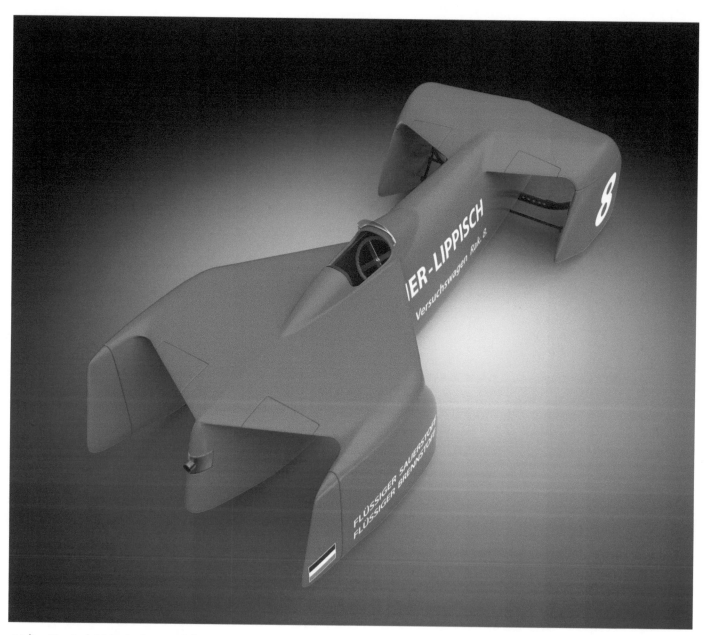

Valier-Lippisch Vehicle 2 was of the *Ente* or canard configuration, with a small wing mounted on the nose and a larger wing placed aft to provide downforce and improve longitudinal stability at high speeds.

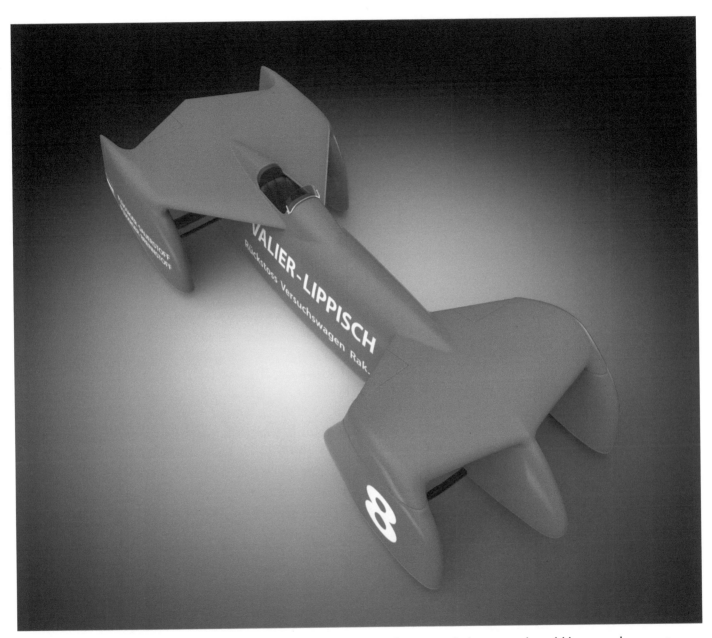

Vehicle 2 had the most modern-looking configuration of the three Valier-Lippisch designs and would have made a spectacular sight on the test track.

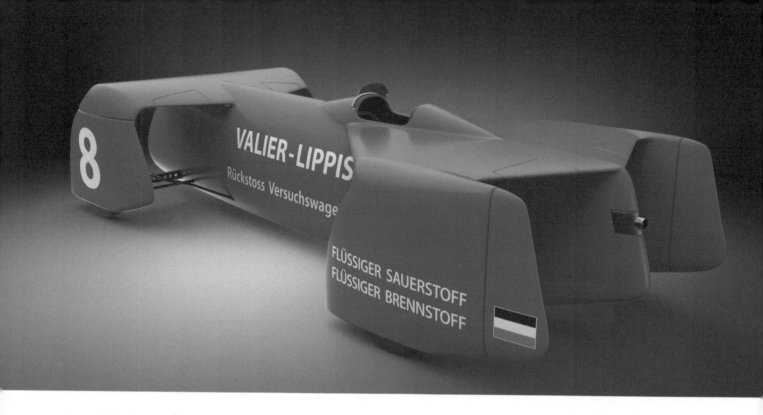

VALIER-LIPPIS
Rückstoss Versuchswage

FLÜSSIGER SAUERSTOFF
FLÜSSIGER BRENNSTOFF

8

However, the employment of rockets as a primary form of automobile propulsion had a much more limited future, being restricted to the occasional speed record attempt and spectacular demonstrations at drag races. Valier had a rather optimistic view of rocketry's potential, and he was certainly proven right with regards to its role in spaceflight and warfare. For obvious reasons, rocket engines have proven to be impractical for general road use and will likely remain so for the foreseeable future.

TOP: Rear view of Valier-Lippisch Vehicle 2 highlighting the twin rudders and central rocket exhaust.

OPPOSITE: Artist's impression of Valier-Lippisch Vehicle 3, which featured prominent vertical fins fore and aft, as well as a large delta wing for which Lippisch would later become famous.

Notes on the Artist's Impressions

There was poor agreement between the available top, side and front views in the patent, making the 3D modeling work especially challenging. I relied mainly upon the side views in the construction of the models, with the top and front views being modified as necessary.

The patent indicates that the configurations were suitable for both rocket and conventional power plants; because of Valier's association with the designs, I decided to make all three versions rocket-powered, specifically the liquid rocket engine used in the Pietsch-Heylandt rocket car of 1931. This was an improved version of the engine Valier had been developing before his death. The size, shape and place-

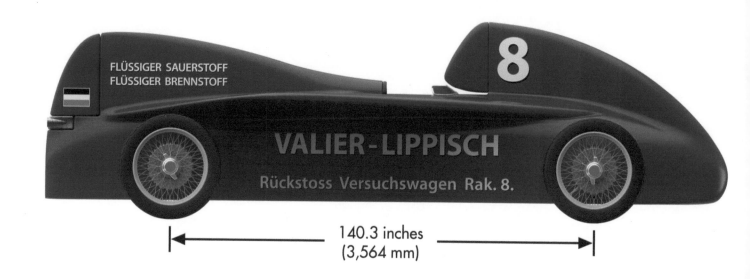

FLÜSSIGER SAUERSTOFF
FLÜSSIGER BRENNSTOFF

VALIER-LIPPISCH

Rückstoss Versuchswagen Rak. 8.

140.3 inches
(3,564 mm)

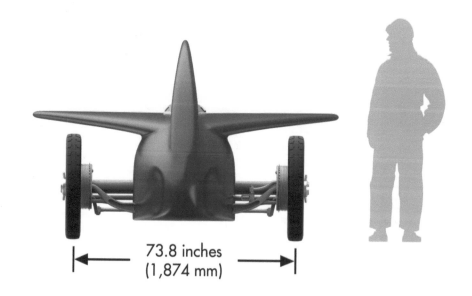

73.8 inches
(1,874 mm)

Note: I estimated the dimensions based on an overall tire diameter of 32.28 inches (820 mm)—the same size of tire used on a reproduction of the Opel RAK.2. Actual size of the design is unknown.

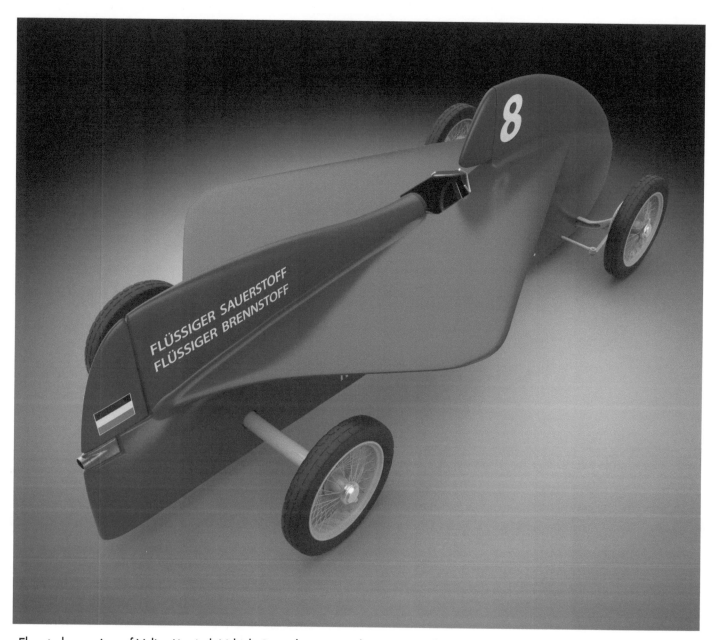

Elevated rear view of Valier-Lippisch Vehicle 3 emphasizing its large arrow-shaped wing; the configuration was based on Lippisch's pioneering work developing tailless aircraft and gliders.

While the forward vision of the driver was not as poor as in Vehicle 1, it still wasn't ideal, with the view being partially blocked by the leading edge of the delta wing and the thick vertical fin immediately in front.

ment of the rocket exhaust is based on drawings of the Pietsch-Heylandt vehicle. The liquid rocket engine was far more efficient in terms of thrust-to-weight ratio than the solid fuel Sander rockets used in the earlier Opel RAK.2.

The estimated size of the Valier-Lippisch vehicles was based on an overall tire diameter of 32.28 inches (820 mm), the diameter of the tires used on an official replica of the Opel RAK.2.[2] All three vehicles feature a speculative suspension, axle and brake arrangement inspired by the Mercedes SSK; I assumed that the leaf springs and shock absorbers were hidden within the body envelope. The windscreens of

Vehicles 1 & 2 are patterned after the Mercedes W25 Silver Arrow, while that of Vehicle 3 is a custom vee-screen. All three vehicles have rather cramped cockpits, necessitating a small diameter steering wheel and a recessed instrument panel.

The markings are a combination of those worn both by the Opel RAK.2 and the Valier-Heylandt Rak.7. I assumed that if one of these Valier-Lippisch designs had been built, it would have been designated *Raketenwagen 8* (Rak.8) in the sequence—hence the large "8" decal on each vehicle. *Rückstoss Versuchswagen* can be translated as "Experimental Thrust Vehicle;" *Flüssiger Sauerstoff* is liquid oxygen and *Flüssiger Brennstoff* is liquid fuel. The German flag decal is the one used on the Opel RAK.2; interestingly, this is the old imperial

TOP: Rear view of Valier-Lippisch Vehicle 3 showing the aft rudder and rocket nozzle. This is the most speculative of the three models in this chapter, as only a top view of the configuration is shown in the patent.

flag and not the official black-red-yellow flag of the Weimar era. The overall color schemes are based on earlier rocket-propelled vehicles developed by Valier. The area immediately around the rocket nozzle is left unpainted on all vehicles, due to the extreme temperatures produced by the thrust of the motor. The unique issues of modeling each configuration are discussed in the following paragraphs.

Valier-Lippisch Vehicle 1

This 3D model is based on the configuration shown in Abbildungen 1, 4 and 6 of the patent; for sake of convenience, it is referred to as Vehicle 1. Unfortunately, there were significant discrepancies between the side and front views in the profile of the front wing stub; the side view shows a thin airfoil, while the front view shows one with a very thick root. I experimented with both versions and found that I could better match the outlines of the top and side views with the thinner airfoil, so I adopted it. Regarding the top view, I had to move the horizontal surfaces and the cockpit aft to better match the side view.

Forward vision would have been appallingly bad for the driver, being obstructed by both the horizontal and vertical surfaces. However, as the vehicle was probably intended only for research and record-breaking, the poor visibility may not have been a great concern. The addition of the rocket engine necessitated division of the rudder into two separate surfaces to accommodate the exhaust nozzle. The black color scheme is inspired by the one worn by the Opel RAK.2.

Valier-Lippisch Vehicle 2

This digital model is based on Abbildungen 2, 5 and 7 of the patent. As with Vehicle 1, there were significant discrepancies between these views, so I modeled it to closely match the side view and modified the top and front views as necessary. This resulted in both a reduction in area and alteration to the geometry of the horizontal wing surfaces. The resulting vehicle is the most modern looking one of the three configurations shown in the patent. The red color scheme is inspired by the Opel-Sander RAK.3 rail vehicle of 1928.

Valier-Lippisch Vehicle 3

The third and final configuration is based on Abbildung 3 of the patent, a top view. Side and front views were lacking, so I created speculative ones based on those of Vehicle 1, which was of similar concept. As with that configuration, forward vision would have been mediocre. The layout anticipates the General Motors Firebird I gas turbine-powered car of 1953, both being tailless deltas looking more at home in the air than on the ground. The blue-grey color scheme is based on the Valier-Heylandt Rak.7, which survives in the Deutsches Museum in Munich.

MILLER-OLDFIELD LAND SPEED RECORD CAR

1932

The Miller-Oldfield Land Speed Record Car, also known as the "Straight-A-Way Car," was a last ditch, long shot effort to save the Miller automobile company from bankruptcy. Harry Miller was a legendary designer and builder of American race cars whose innovations included the development of aluminum pistons, the first front wheel drive race car and the first four wheel drive race car. Miller racers won the Indianapolis 500 nine times, while other cars fitted with his engines won it three additional times in the interwar period. While business was good in the 1920s, by the early 1930s Miller's financial fortunes had taken a turn for the worse.

Barney Oldfield was a famous American race car driver and showman who had traveled throughout the United States in a series of timed runs and match races in the first two decades of the twentieth century, earning him a small fortune. Oldfield set a world speed record of 131.724 mph (211.989 km/h) with his "Blitzen Benz" race car at Daytona Beach, Florida on March 16, 1910. Oldfield's association with

Miller began in 1917, when he successfully raced the Miller *Golden Submarine* against the legendary Ralph DePalma in a series of match races at Milwaukee, Wisconsin. This formidable and beautiful vehicle put Miller on the map as a builder of race cars. Oldfield retired from auto racing in 1918, spending the 1920s involved in various projects in the entertainment and automotive fields. By 1932, Oldfield was ready to re-enter the racing arena, with the Miller-Oldfield Land Speed Record Car being his ticket back in.

Miller and Oldfield released details of their proposed record vehicle in May 1932. It was a long and narrow design with an aerodynamic body and streamlined underpan. The driver was situated well to the rear in a closed cabin with a removable hatch. At the time, the record was held by Briton Malcolm Campbell and his Campbell-Napier-Railton Blue Bird with a speed of 253.97 mph (408.73 km/h). The Mill-

OPPOSITE: Artist's impression of the Miller-Oldfield Land Speed Record Car project of 1932, a huge vehicle powered by a 24-cylinder engine capable of 3,000 bhp.

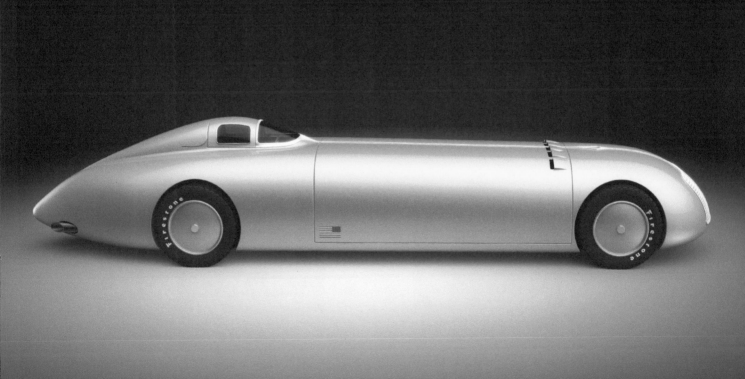

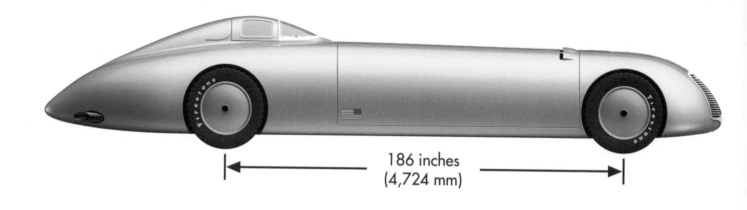

186 inches
(4,724 mm)

61.1 inches
(1,553 mm)

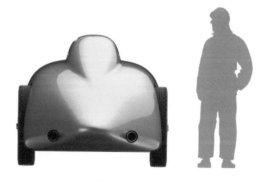

er-Oldfield car was designed to take the record back from the British and also save the Miller company. It was capable of speeds well over 200 mph (321.87 km/h) in endurance record attempts at Bonneville and was powered by a new 3,000 bhp Roots-blown V-24 "marine" engine weighing 2,300 lbs (1,043 kg). This was likely the same engine proposed to the U.S. Army Air Corps on Miller's behalf by Preston Tucker a few months before. The engine featured three individual carburetors—one for each supercharger. It was four wheel drive with typical Miller fore-and-aft de Dion suspension and paired quarter elliptics. The vehicle had a wheel base of 186

inches (4,724 mm), with an overall length of 316 in (8,026 mm). Measurement of the blueprint indicates a front wheel track of 61.1 inches (1,553 mm). The overall weight was a staggering 6,500 lbs (2,948 kg).[3]

No investors came forward to finance the construction of this huge and expensive vehicle, which died a quiet death and quickly slipped into obscurity. Harry Miller went bankrupt in 1933; his business was purchased by Miller employee Fred Offenhauser, who continued development of the original Miller engine under the Offenhauser name, racing it successfully into the 1980s. Miller partnered with Preston Tucker and developed various projects together, including several race cars and an armored car for the military. However, Miller never found the degree of success he had previously enjoyed,

TOP: Aft view of the Miller-Oldfield Straight-A-Way Car showing its tapered rear end and one of its large exhaust pipes.

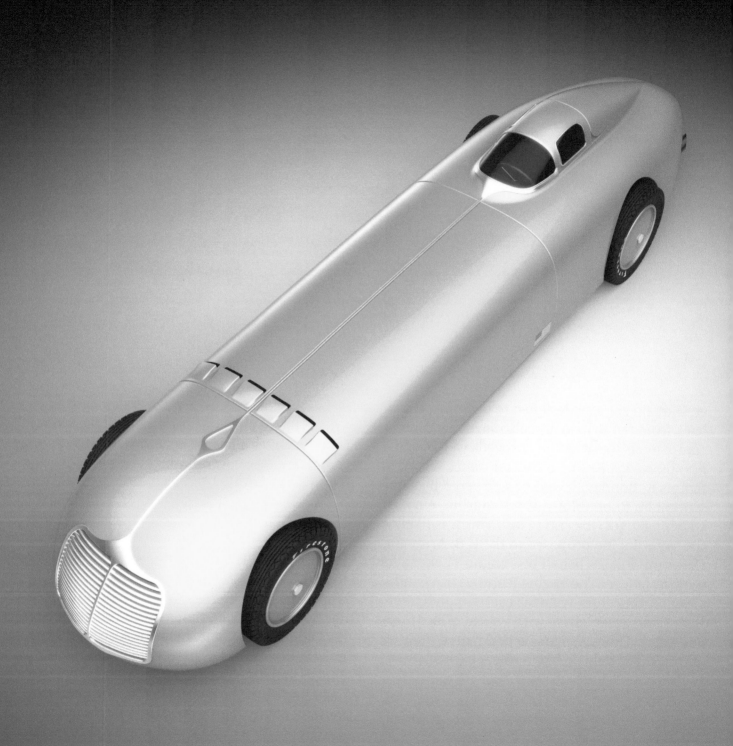

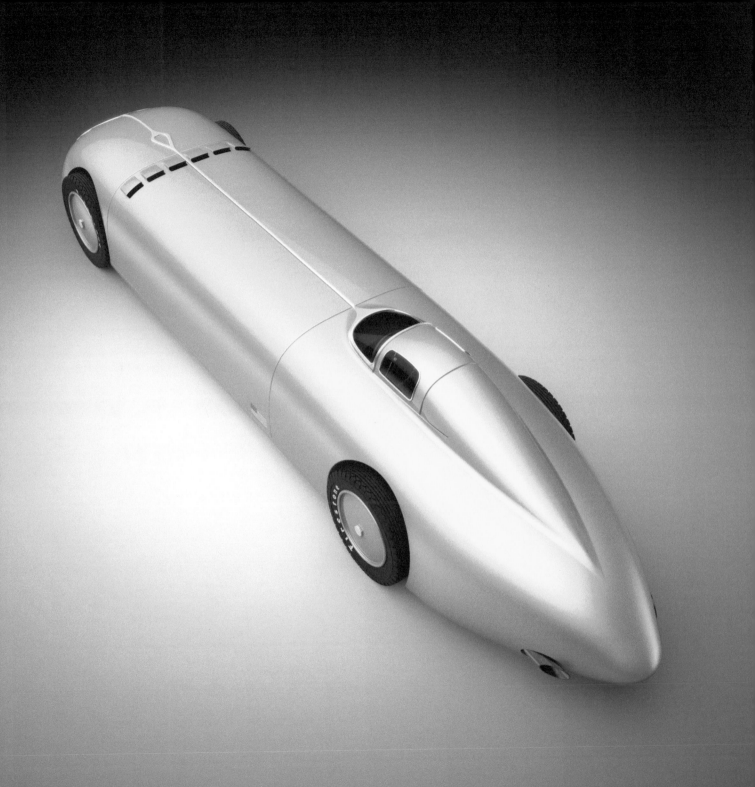

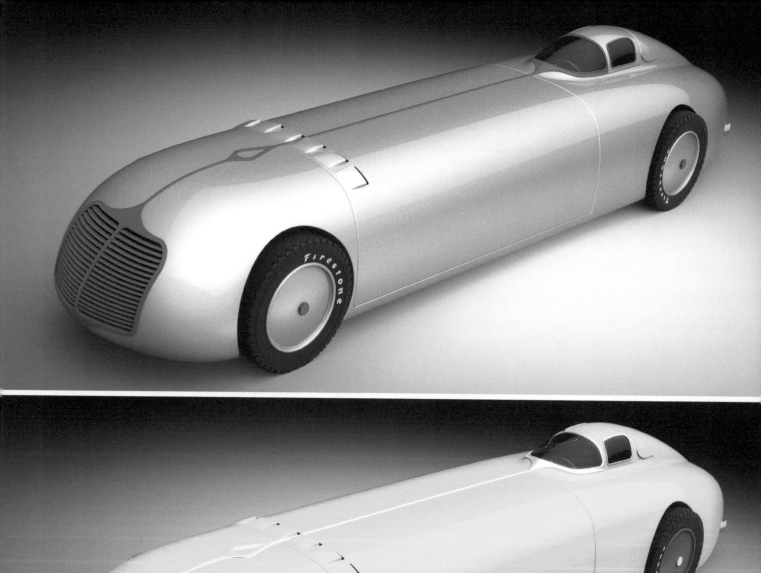
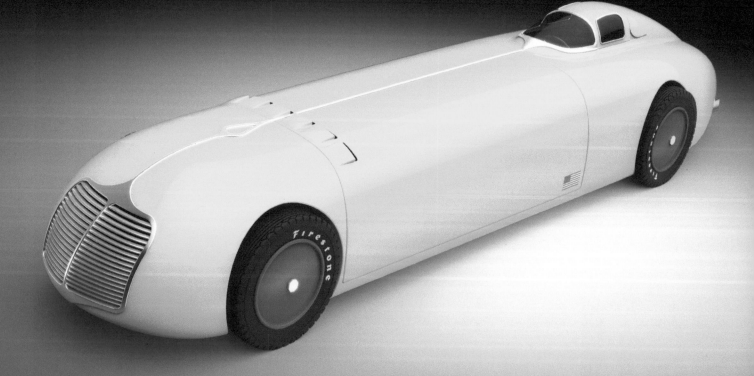

passing away May 3, 1943 in Detroit, Michigan, with Tucker helping cover the cost of the funeral for Miller's widow.[4]

After the failure of the Miller-Oldfield record car to attract investors, Barney Oldfield returned to the movie business, advising on and even appearing in several pictures, including *The Blonde Comet* of 1941. He died of a heart attack on October 4, 1946 in Beverly Hills, California.[5]

Notes on the Artist's Impressions

The 3D model was based on a blueprint in Mark Dees' superlative book *The Miller Dynasty*. Unfortunately, the drawing lacked a front view, so I created cross sections based on surviving photos of a display model used to promote the project. The blueprint otherwise provided very good reference for modeling the vehicle, except for some minor discrepancies in the placement of the front grill.

The overall color scheme of gold with chrome trim is inspired by the original *Golden Submarine* of 1917. It was the first collaboration between Miller and Oldfield, one that achieved public prominence, so it seemed possible that Miller might have wanted to associate his new vehicle with the success of the old one. However, the gold color was also associated with the

British *Golden Arrow* record breaker of 1929, so perhaps Miller would have chosen an alternate scheme, such as the silver and red combination depicted on the opposite page. This is based on photos of the aforementioned display model, which appears to have been silver with dark-colored trim, possibly black or red. Finally, I present the Miller-Oldfield in a yellow and red scheme inspired by the colors worn by a surviving Miller race car. I did not apply any large sponsor decals to the color schemes, as it wasn't common in this period to prominently feature such logos on race cars. I did add a small American flag on two of the schemes, as I think Miller was patriotic and wanted to capture the speed record not only for his company but also for the United States. The Firestone tires are similar to the ones used on the *Mormon Meteor III*, a speed record car built in 1937.

PREVIOUS SPREAD: Elevated front and rear views of the Miller-Oldfield Land Speed Record Car emphasizing its very long nose and narrow wheel track.

OPPOSITE: Alternate color schemes for the Miller-Oldfield; how it actually would have been painted is anyone's guess.

GEE-BEE ATLANTA RACING CAR

1933

The "Gee-Bee" name is usually associated with a series of fast but dangerous aircraft which dominated air racing in the early 1930s; far more obscure is its connection to an unconventional three-wheel race car design from 1933. The air racers were produced by Granville Brothers Aircraft of Springfield, Massachusetts, which was founded by Zantford "Grannie" Granville and his brothers in 1925. Initially an aircraft repair business, Granville built its first aircraft in 1929, the Model A two-seat biplane. This was followed by a series of "Sportsters" which would evolve from relatively conventional commercial airplanes into radical and hazardous bullet-like racers which briefly dominated interwar air racing and cost the lives of several pilots.

Among private aircraft manufacturers, the Granvilles were considered gifted engineers who were not afraid to adopt the latest aerodynamic theories of the day. They were among the earliest companies to regularly use wind tunnel testing to refine their designs, which were conceived with the highest performance standards in mind. The resulting aircraft were tubby manned projectiles with wingspans greater than the length of their fuselages, resulting in high landing speeds and tricky handling characteristics that only the most skilled of pilots could master.[6]

Their most famous creation was likely the R-1 Super Sportster, which was piloted by Jimmy Doolittle to win the Thompson Trophy Race on September 5, 1932. This would prove to be their last major success; a series of highly publicized accidents and deteriorating finances resulted in the company declaring bankruptcy towards the end of 1933. Refusing to give up, Grannie Granville, Howell Miller and Donald DeLackner opened a consulting engineering firm in New York City. The company's first project was not an airplane but an automobile, specifically an Indianapolis 500 racer. Grannie had attended the 1933 Memorial Day classic and believed he could improve upon existing race car design, which was not optimal from an aerodynamic standpoint, lacking streamlined underpans and having open, drag-inducing driving compartments. In response, the three men designed the "Atlanta," a streamlined

---

OPPOSITE: Artist's impressions of the Gee-Bee Atlanta three-wheel race car of 1934, Granville's sole known foray into the automotive field.

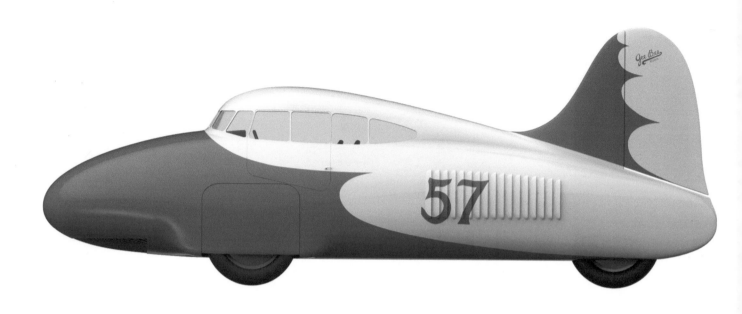

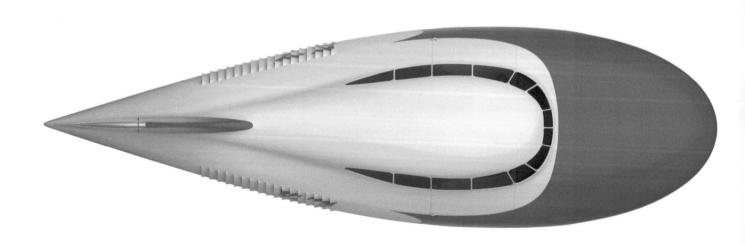

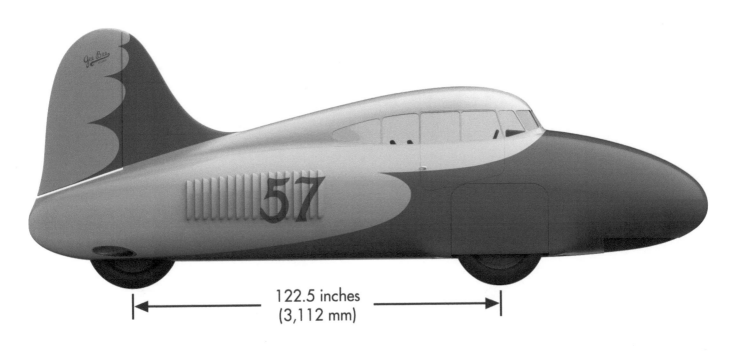

122.5 inches
(3,112 mm)

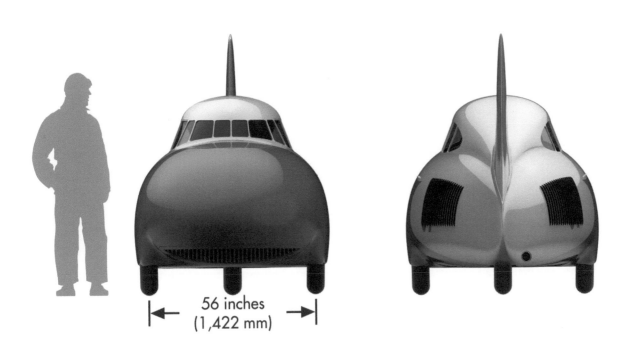

56 inches
(1,422 mm)

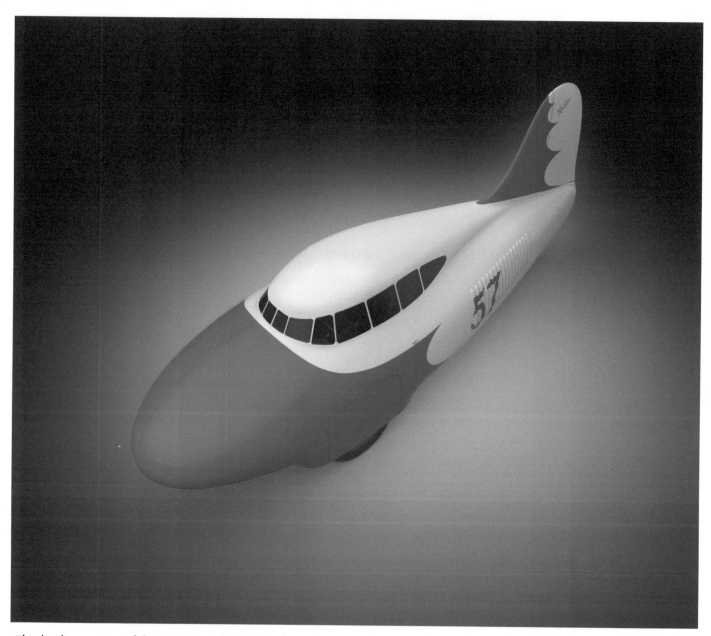

This bird's eye view of the Gee-Bee Atlanta reveals its classic teardrop shape and segmented windshield, which was patterned after aircraft like the Douglas DC-2. Granville and his fellow engineers made a point of enclosing the cabin to reduce drag and improve driver safety.

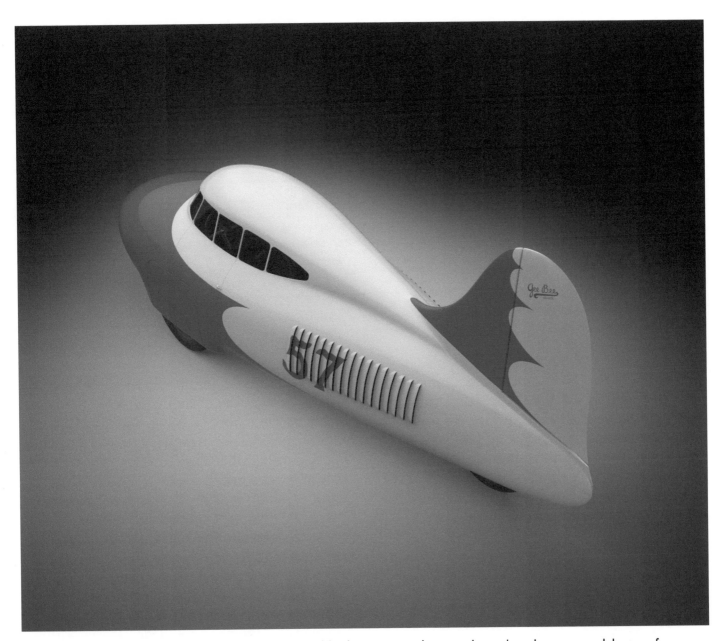

The Atlanta's three-wheel layout resulted in a remarkably slippery, aerodynamic shape, but also prevented the type from racing at the Indianapolis Speedway, which only permitted four-wheel vehicles. Realization of this fact in late 1933 quickly killed the project.

automobile powered by a standard unmodified Ford V-8 with an estimated top speed of 140 miles per hour. The three-wheeled car was of a teardrop shape like the R-1 aircraft with a prominent vertical fin and rudder. The engine drove the front wheels and the underside of the vehicle was covered to reduce drag. The enclosed driver's compartment had a segmented

TOP: Rear view of the Gee-Bee Atlanta emphasizing its aircraft-like vertical tail and overall streamlined form. Exhaust and louver details are speculative.

OPPOSITE: Alternate color schemes for the Atlanta based on earlier Gee-Bee Aircraft. The yellow and black livery is inspired by the Model "Z" Super Sportster, which won the Thompson Trophy in 1931. The Blue-Red-White scheme is inspired by the Model "D" Sportster, which won the Williams Trophy at the Cleveland Air Races in 1931.

windshield heavily influenced by contemporary aircraft design. DeLackner completed the final layout on December 14, 1933. Technical specifications included an overall length of 227 inches (5,766 mm); a wheelbase of 122.5 inches (3,112 mm); a front wheel track of 56 inches (1,422 mm); an empty weight of 1,750 lbs (794 kg); and a racing weight of 2,500 lbs (1,134 kg).

The Atlanta was designed to compete in the 1934 Indianapolis 500. Fate intervened when Captain Eddie Rickenbacker, president of the Indianapolis Speedway, visited the office of Granville, Miller and DeLackner and examined the plans for their radical racer. He regretfully informed them that only four-wheel vehicles were permitted to race at the Speedway and the Atlanta would not be allowed to compete, abruptly ending the project.[7]

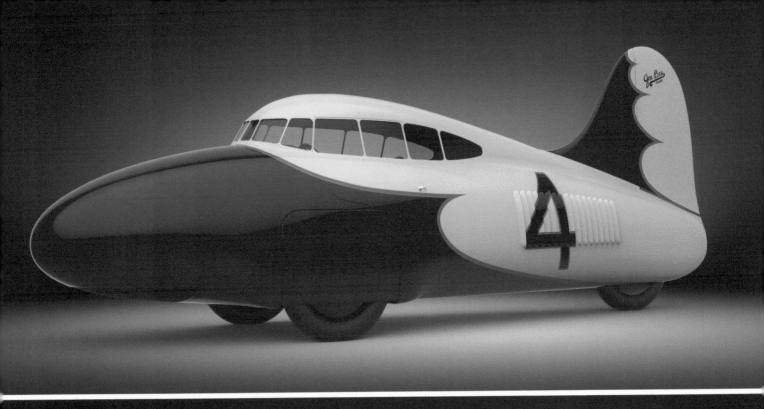
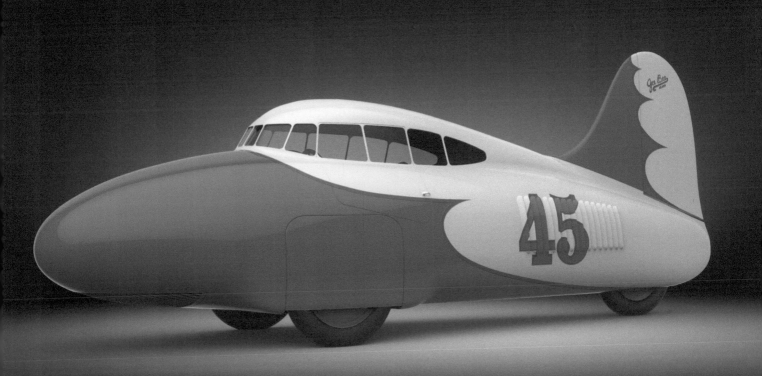

Notes on the Artist's Impressions

The 3D model is based on a set of plans found in *The Gee Bee Racers: A Legacy of Speed* by Charles Mendenhall. There was relatively good agreement between the views, though the plans lacked detail in certain areas. I assumed it was a mid-engine design and added a grill underneath the nose to provide cooling air to the radiator. I added louvers along the sides to provide ventilation for the engine area. I placed a streamlined exhaust pipe at the aft end of the vehicle on the right side. How these and other engineering details would have actually been resolved by Granville and his associates can only be speculated upon, given the brief existence of the project.

The scalloped red and white color scheme is based on the original drawing of the car as well as the iconic Gee-Bee Model R-1 Super Sportster, winner of the 1932 Thompson Trophy. Some other possible color schemes are shown on pages 77-78. These are based on earlier models of Gee-Bee aircraft, specifically the Model "Z" Super Sportster and Model "D" Sportster.

TOP: This brown and beige combination is inspired by an alternate color scheme which may have been worn by the Model "D" Sportster. There is some disagreement about the colors of the more minor Gee-Bee aircraft, as original photos of them are almost all in black and white. In any case, the Granvilles probably would have invented an entirely new color scheme to suit their car had it left the drawing board.

MICKL RECORD CAR WITH WING

1937

The Mercedes-Benz T80 was a huge six-wheel vehicle designed by Dr. Ferdinand Porsche to break the world land speed record for the Third Reich. The project was the brainchild of Hans Stuck, a famous German race car driver who wanted to end British domination of the record and bring it to his home country. Stuck eventually won the support of Hitler, a motorsports enthusiast who recognized the propaganda value of the project. Work began in 1937 under the leadership of Porsche. The initial speed target was 342 mph (550 km/h), but by late 1939 this had been raised to an impressive 470 mph (750 km/h) in the wake of several more successful land speed record runs by the British.

The T80 was powered by a prototype Daimler-Benz DB 603 inverted V12 aircraft engine tuned to produce 3,000 hp (2,200 kW). With a displacement of 44.52 liters, this was the largest engine of its type produced in Germany during WW II. The T80 was over 26 ft (8 m) long and weighed 2.98 tons (2.7 metric tons). It was built at a cost of 600,000 *Reichsmarks* (US $25.8 million as of 2016), a staggering sum for the period.

The Mercedes-Benz T80 was heavily streamlined, with an enclosed cockpit, low sloping hood, rounded fenders, and tandem rear wheel fairings which formed elongated vertical tail booms. Two stubby wings were located midway along the sides of the vehicle to provide downforce and longitudinal stability; these were likely inspired by the wings of the Opel RAK.2 rocket car discussed previously. The T80 had a drag coefficient of 0.18, which is impressive even by modern standards.

The record attempt was planned for January 1940, with Hans Stuck driving the T80 over a special stretch of the *Reichsautobahn* Berlin—Halle/Leipzig, which passed south of Dessau. The outbreak of the war on September 1, 1939 precluded the run, and the T80 was eventually placed into storage in Kärnten, Austria. Surviving the war, the vehicle was moved to the Mercedes-Benz Museum in Stuttgart, Germany, where it is on permanent display in unrestored condition.[8]

The aerodynamics of the T80 were the product of work by Josef Mickl, an Austrian aeronautical and mechanical engineer. During WW I, he was head of the *Oeffag* design office, which built seaplanes for the Austro-Hungarian Navy. The Treaty of Saint-Germain in 1919 se-

verely restricted the Austrian aviation industry, forcing Mickl to seek work in the automotive sector. He found a job with Dr. Porsche at the Austro-Daimler company, where he helped design the structure and the engine of the Sascha racing car, which won the Targa Florio in 1922. Later that year, he was invited to Yugoslavia, where he worked as an aviation expert and designer, eventually becoming technical director and construction manager at the Ikarus aircraft factory, where he helped develop several aircraft types. By 1931 he was employed at the Porsche design office in Stuttgart, where he worked on improving automobile aerodynamics, in particular the racing and record cars of Auto Union. He was also involved in the design of the Volkswagen Beetle.[9]

In the course of developing the aerodynamics of the T80, numerous configurations were studied, one of which is the subject of this chapter. This particular design was patented May 8, 1937 by Mickl and the Porsche company. Receiving German patent no. 698,052, the invention concerned a race or record car with a streamlined body; a rear wing to increase downforce; and substantial vertical surfaces to support the wing and provide lateral stability.

Previous attempts at increasing vehicle downforce had resulted in an increase in the length of the vehicle and/or the necessity of making the supporting structure of the wing surfaces very strong, causing an increase of vehicle construction costs and overall weight. The Mickl Record Car promised to increase downforce and lateral stability at reduced cost and only a minor increase in vehicle weight. Lateral stabilization was achieved with relatively small vertical surfaces, while downforce was achieved without increasing the length of the vehicle.

When viewed from above, the Mickl Record Car had a wedge-like shape, wider at the front than at the rear. Like the final T80 design, it was a six-wheel vehicle with a heavily streamlined, aerodynamic body. A two-piece wing was mounted on a pair of streamlined supports, which were rigidly attached to the tandem wheel fairings. The wing increased the load on the rear wheels, while the vertical supports enhanced lateral stability. The combination of the streamlined body, prominent rear wheel fairings, wing, and its vertical supports created a sort of jet-like nozzle at the rear of the vehicle, which helped reduce drag and increase the overall speed.

Circular endplates were added to the ends of the wing to enhance the downforce effect. The wing could be used as an effective airbrake surface if designed to swivel on the transverse axis of the vehicle. The swiveling of the wing could also help regulate the downforce effect. There were several options for the wing: it could be rigidly attached to the vertical supports, with only the aft section being adjustable; it could be fully adjustable; or it could be rigidly attached with no articulation. Mickl proposed making the wing's angle of attack manually adjustable by the driver or automatically adjusted by a mechanical device. Whether the vehicle was front, rear or all-wheel drive did not affect the claims made in the patent.

The idea of using airfoil surfaces to

OPPOSITE: Artist's impressions of the Mickl Record Car of 1937, an early configuration of the Mercedes-Benz T80 featuring a large rear wing mounted on the rear wheel fairings.

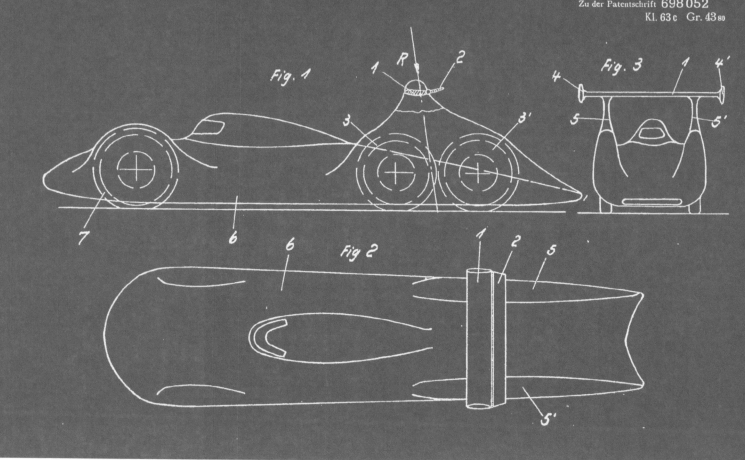

Zu der Patentschrift 698052
Kl. 63c Gr. 43₈₀

Fig. 1

Fig. 3

Fig 2

TOP: Patent drawings of the Mickl Record Car dating from 1937.

generate downforce began with the Opel RAK.2 rocket-propelled vehicle of 1928. Interestingly, this was also the solution chosen by Porsche for the final configuration of the T80. The Mickl Record Car may not have had enough downforce generated at the front of the car, causing it to be passed over when it came time to finalize the T80 configuration; this is insinuated in the Sawatzki patent covered in the following chapter. The idea of using a rear-mounted wing to generate downforce would basically remain dormant until 1965, with the introduction of the Chaparral 2C. It wouldn't revolutionize motorsports until 1968, when airfoil surfaces were added to the Lotus 49 formula one car, which would eventually win 12 grand prix races. The rear-mounted wing is now a fixture of both F1 and sports car design. Hopefully Mickl will someday receive wider recognition for this important contribution to automobile aerodynamics.

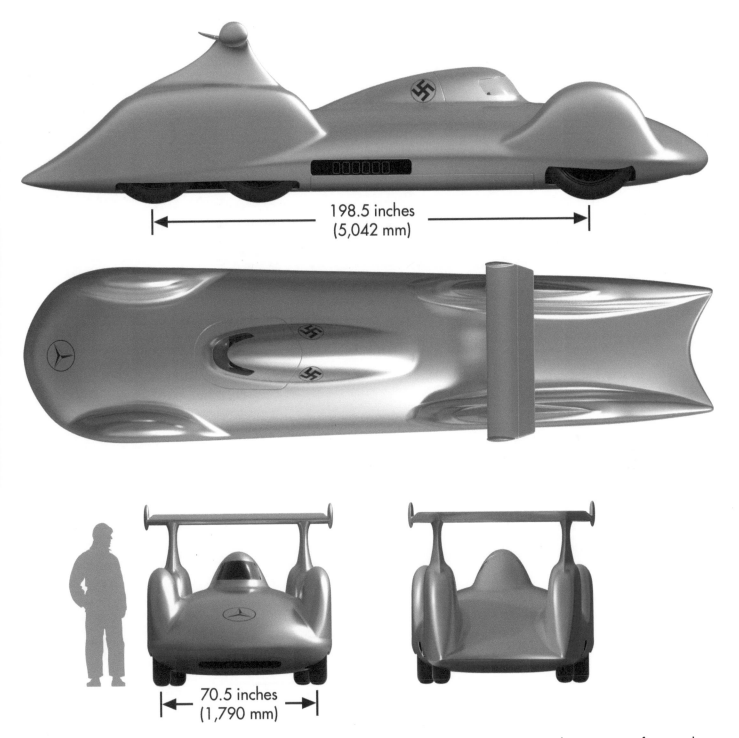

198.5 inches
(5,042 mm)

70.5 inches
(1,790 mm)

Note: I estimated the dimensions based on an overall tire diameter of 46.44 inches (1,180 mm)—the same size of tire used on the Mercedes-Benz T80. Actual size of the vehicle is unknown.

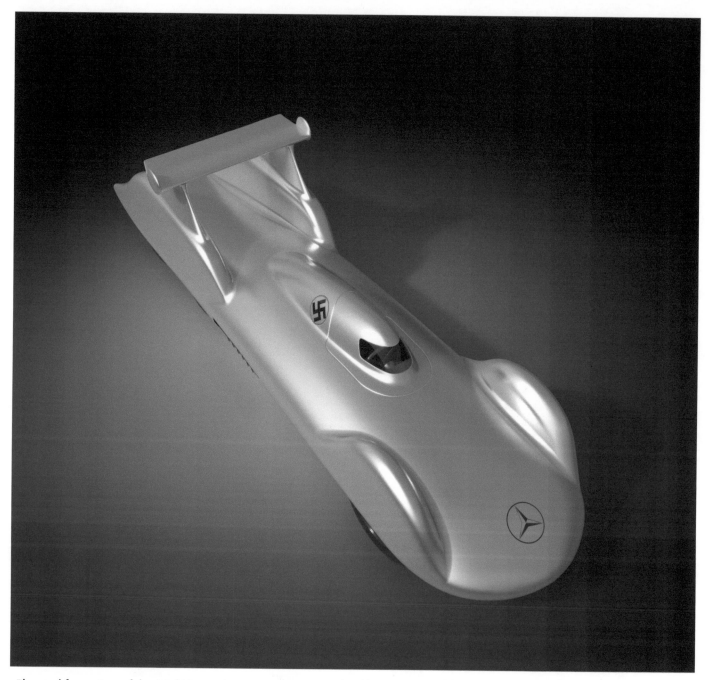

Elevated front view of the Mickl Record Car revealing its wedge-like shape, which was wider at the front than at the rear. Like the T80, it was a large six-wheel vehicle with prominent fairings which improved lateral stability at high speeds.

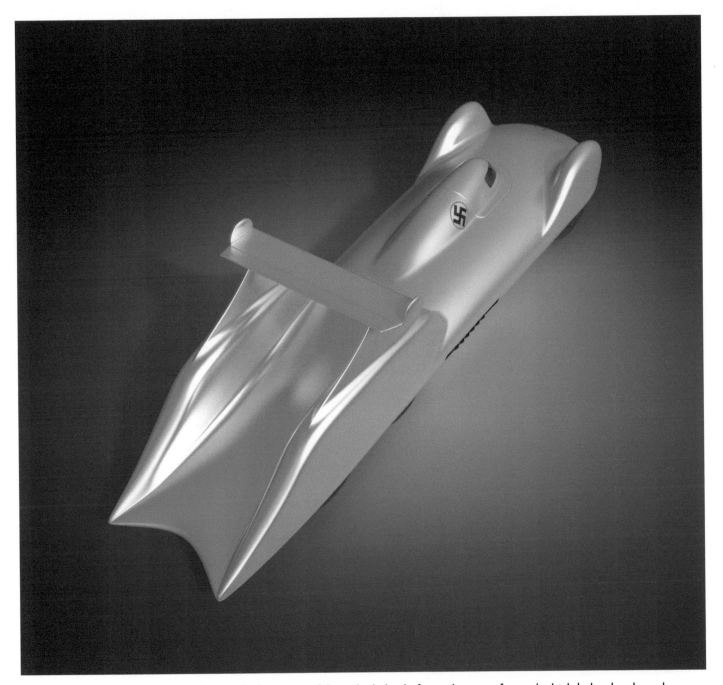

The rear wing, tail booms, and flattened aft portion of the vehicle body formed a sort of tunnel which helped reduce drag and increase the overall speed of the Mickl Record Car. Endplates were added to the wing to improve the downforce effect.

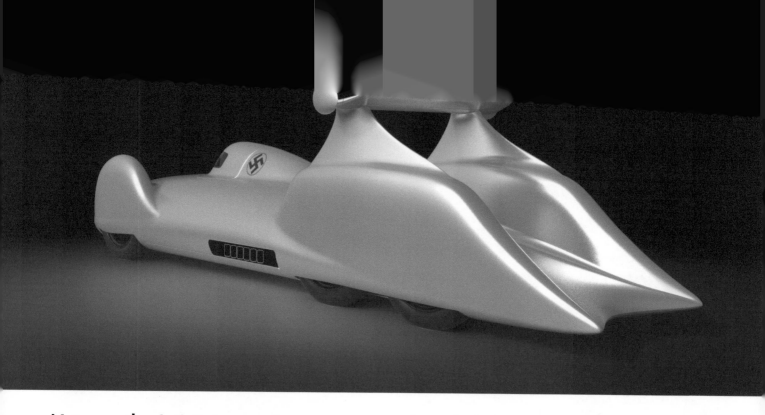

Notes on the Artist's Impressions

In estimating the size of the Mickl Record Car, it was assumed to have the same overall tire diameter as the actual T80—46.44 inches (1,180 mm). This resulted in an overall length of 311.9 inches (7,922 mm); a wheelbase of 198.5 inches (5,042 mm); and a front wheel track of 70.5 inches (1,790 mm). The design and placement of the exhaust stacks were based on that of the T80, as I assumed that the Mickl Record Car would have been powered by the same Daimler-Benz DB 603 aircraft engine. Other details borrowed from the T80 include the spoked wheels, the outline of the cockpit cover, and details of the interior. Like the other Mercedes-Benz "Silver Arrows," the Mickl design is painted silver overall with the famous three-pointed star on the nose. The swastika decal is based on one worn by the Mercedes-Benz *Rekordwagen* of 1936-37. Perhaps a more colorful scheme would have been adopted for the record attempt, but I felt it was prudent to adopt a conservative color scheme for which there was historical precedent.

TOP: Rear view of the Mickl Record Car showing the tandem rear wheels and exhaust stack, which was patterned after that of the Mercedes-Benz T80.

SAWATZKI RECORD CAR WITH AIR BRAKES

1939

The vehicle presented in this chapter is another configuration studied during the development of the Mercedes-Benz T80 land speed record car; it is based on two German patents. The first, no. 762,588, established the overall shape of the vehicle, which was patented June 6, 1939 and titled *Vehicle Body for High Speeds, Especially for Racing and Record Vehicles*. Engineers Ewald Sawatzki and Christian Schmid of the Research Institute for Automotive Industry and Vehicle Motors at the Technical University in Stuttgart, Germany are listed as the inventors. Little information is available on these men, who are evidently more obscure figures than Mickl and Porsche.

According to the document, existing vehicles started to become unsafe at high speeds when a certain speed on the road was exceeded, and this effect was not dependent solely on the ground condition or tire grip. This instability grew with increasing speed and was due to the inadequate stability of the vehicle both laterally and longitudinally. Even contemporary race cars were still heavily subjected to the adverse

influence of these forces, making ground adhesion and lateral stability insufficient, although progress in streamlining had improved longitudinal stability.

In the development of the T80, various individual measures had been experimented with to provide a remedy. For example, it had already been proposed to achieve downforce on the rear of the vehicle by attaching a wing to the tail, thus increasing the ground adhesion of the rear wheels. However, this resulted in marginal ground adhesion of the front wheels and a considerable increase in the driving resistance, with no improvement in overall driving safety.

Alternatively, one could give the nose upwardly sloping concave surfaces for improving the ground adhesion of the front wheels. However, this unilateral measure generally worsened driving safety, in particular the direction of travel, as the grip of the rear wheels was greatly reduced.

Other previously studied individual measures, such as the shaping of the nose itself to form a scoop-like, curved concave surface, did

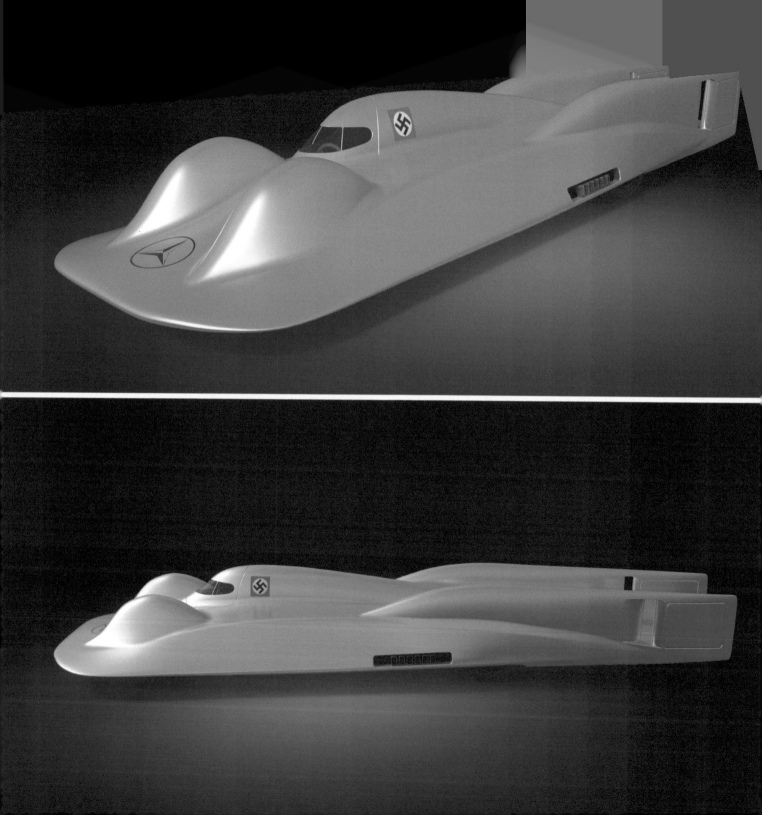

not result in a vehicle which was safe to drive at high speeds. Flattening the tail into a blade-like horizontal surface and gradually raising the contours of the underside of the nose and tail also didn't solve the problem.

While all of the aforementioned measures had produced only unilateral effects and thus worsened the overall behavior of the vehicle, the configuration proposed by Sawatzki and Schmid, by virtue of the unique combination and mutual adaptation of these known features and the use of new innovations, in particular the application of greatly extended concave surfaces along the sides from the shovel-like nose, which on both sides were gradually blended into two vertical tails, succeeded in creating a "perfectly satisfactory" solution to the stability problems encountered by vehicles driven at high speeds.

The main body of the Sawatzki and Schmid design was pike or dolphin-like when viewed from the side. It had prominent fairings over the front and rear wheels, with the aft fairings extending into long vertical tail booms. At the end of the flattened horizontal tail was an adjustable elevator to provide downforce.

The nose sloped upwards concavely and broadened in the horizontal plane beyond the front fenders, blending into the concave side surfaces. These side surfaces gradually merged with the two vertical tail booms formed by the fairings of the rear wheels. The tail itself flattened out into a sharp horizontal edge; like the nose, the bottom side was slightly raised. The long cockpit fairing also gradually blended into the horizontal tail. At the nose, the upwardly curving underside was present both in the longitudinal and transverse directions.

The concave shape of the nose, not only in the forward direction, but also along the sides, caused an improvement in the direction of travel, in addition to an increase in the ground adhesion. This was due to the fact that when driving the vehicle, the resulting air force and side wind was always at an angle opposite to the direction of travel on the nose. The resultant lateral partial force could be divided into two forces acting on the front and rear axles. The force on the front axle always produced a detrimental moment, which caused the vehicle to divert from the direction of travel; the force on the rear axle had the reverse effect, depending on the configuration of the tail. Due to the shaping of the Sawatzki and Schmid design, the rotational force acting on the front axle was substantially reduced by the fact that the lateral surfaces of the nose were inclined and concave. The air stream impinging from the sides onto the front part of the vehicle was then deflected upwards and rearwards. As a result, the lateral force acting as a rotational force was substantially smaller than if the side wall of the nose was, as per convention, vertical or outwardly curved. The vertical component of the lateral force improved the ground adhesion of the wheels. Since the force acting in the front turning direction became smaller, it was possible to make the vertical tail booms smaller and thereby reduce the entire lateral force.

A further advantage of this shaping of the vehicle was that the lower edge, which was formed by the oblique side surfaces of the nose,

---

OPPOSITE: Artist's impressions of the Sawatzki Record Car of 1939, an alternate T80 study that never left the drawing board.

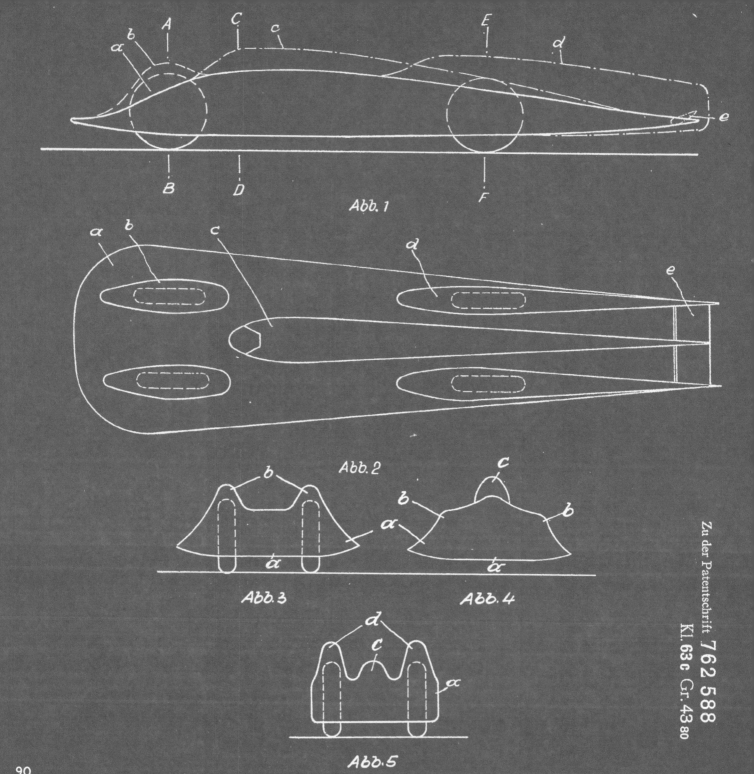

Abb. 1

Abb. 2

Abb. 3

Abb. 4

Abb. 5

Zu der Patentschrift **762 588**
Kl. 63c Gr. 43 80

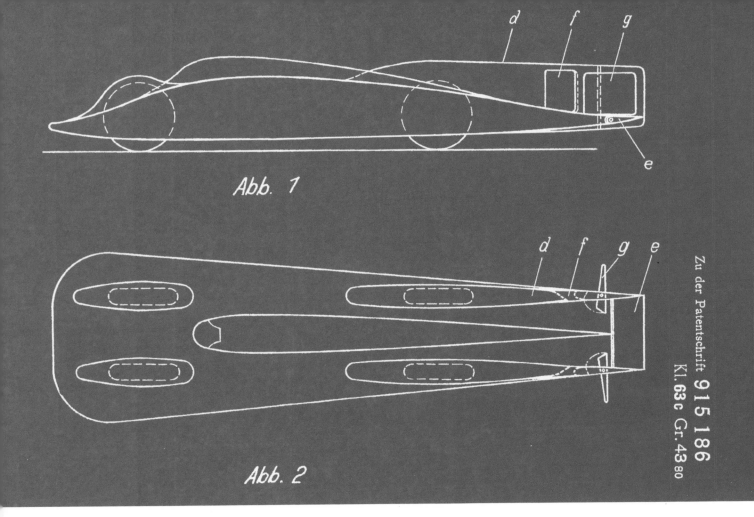

Abb. 1

Abb. 2

Zu der Patentschrift 915 186
Kl. 63 c Gr. 43 80

which ran horizontally or slightly inclined to the roadway, prevented the formation of disturbing boundary vortices, so that despite the end sur-face enlargement there was little or no increase of the actual air resistance.

The elevator built into the tail was able to improve performance with minimal power input. Only a few degrees of adjustment to the rear elevator were sufficient to obtain the desired downforce effect.

The design was further refined with German patent no. 915,186 dated August 8, 1939. Titled *Vehicle Body for High Speeds, Especially for Racing and Record Vehicles*, the patent is only attributed to Sawatzki as the inventor, now

OPPOSITE: Drawings from German patent no. 762,588, an earlier iteration of the car illustrated in this chapter. The cross sections were adapted to the drawings of the later patent in constructing the 3D model.

TOP: Drawings from German patent no. 915,186 showing the Sawatzki Record Car. While similar to the earlier patent, the addition of the large slots and air brakes at the rear of the booms set this design apart.

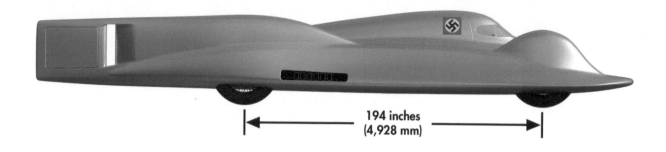

194 inches
(4,928 mm)

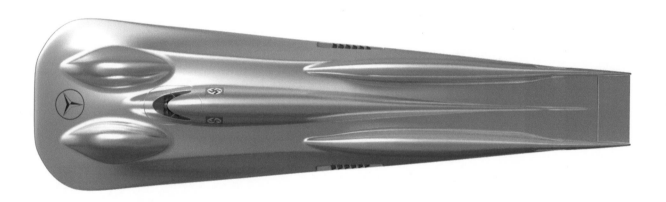

47.6 inches
(1,209 mm)

Note: I estimated the dimensions based on an overall tire diameter of 46.44 inches (1,180 mm)—the same size as the Mercedes-Benz T80. Actual size of the vehicle is unknown.

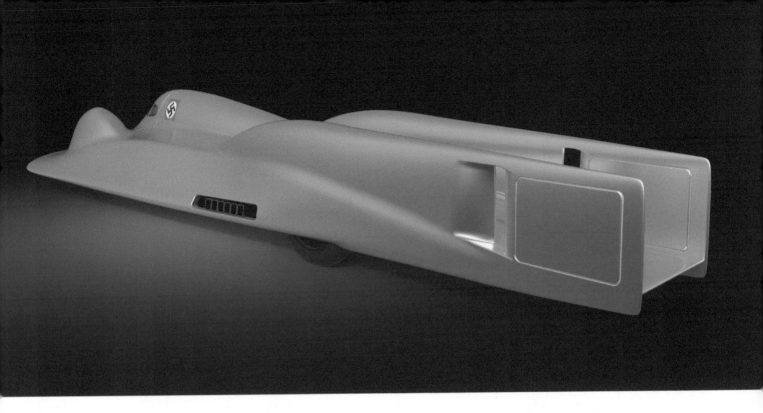

working for Daimler-Benz. The invention relates to a vehicle body for high speed, in particular for racing and record vehicles. The car featured an elevator at the tail and had vertical tail booms arranged on both sides, the rear booms being partially interrupted with prominent slots.

According to the invention, the vehicle was provided with a frame section for accommodating a hinged brake flap behind the slot on each tail boom, and the elevator was coupled to the brake flaps in a mechanical, electrical or other manner in such a way that the acting air pressure on the elevator and tail movement was preserved.

Except for the addition of the slots, large air brakes and a slight change to the contours of the tail booms, the vehicle configuration presented in this patent was quite similar to the previous one.

Why this configuration was passed over is unknown; perhaps it was deemed too large and heavy, or Porsche was skeptical of the air brake-elevator combination. In any case, he chose the more conservative layout for the T80 that now resides in Stuttgart.

Notes on the Artist's Impressions

The 3D model is primarily based on

TOP: Rear view of the Sawatzki Record Car emphasizing its long tail booms and massive air brakes. The slots ahead of the air brakes helped channel air over the rear elevator to enhance the downforce effect.

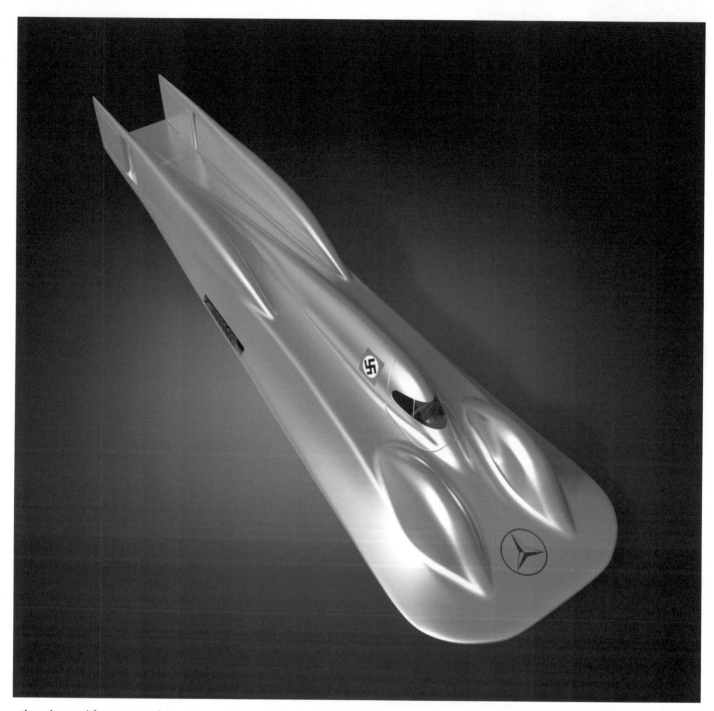

This elevated front view of the Sawatzki Record Car highlights its extreme wedge-like shaping as well as the broad, duck-like nose. Also noteworthy are the concave surfaces along the sides, which enhanced stability and ground adhesion.

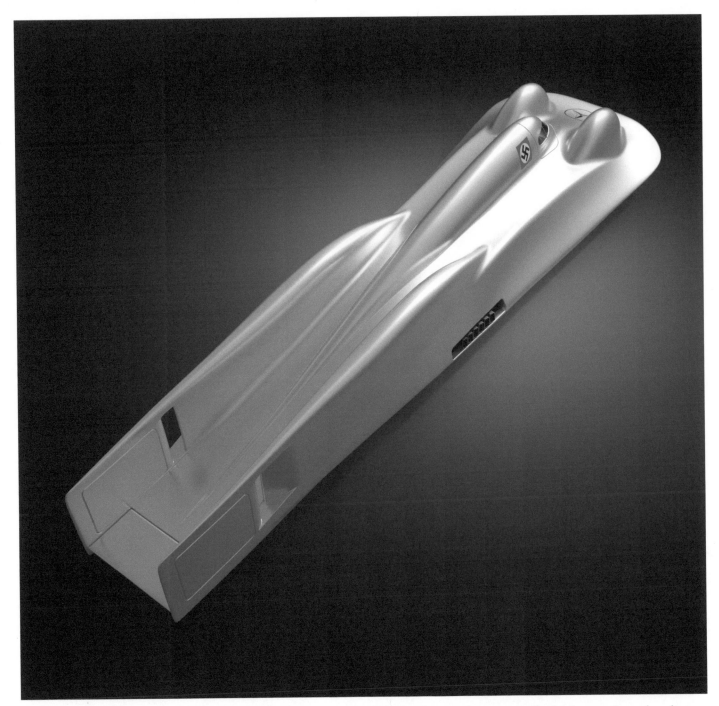

The Sawatzki design was a very long vehicle, with an estimated length of 32.44 ft (9.89 m). The body was shaped to direct air over the rear elevator, which helped provide the downforce necessary to keep the car on the track at high speeds.

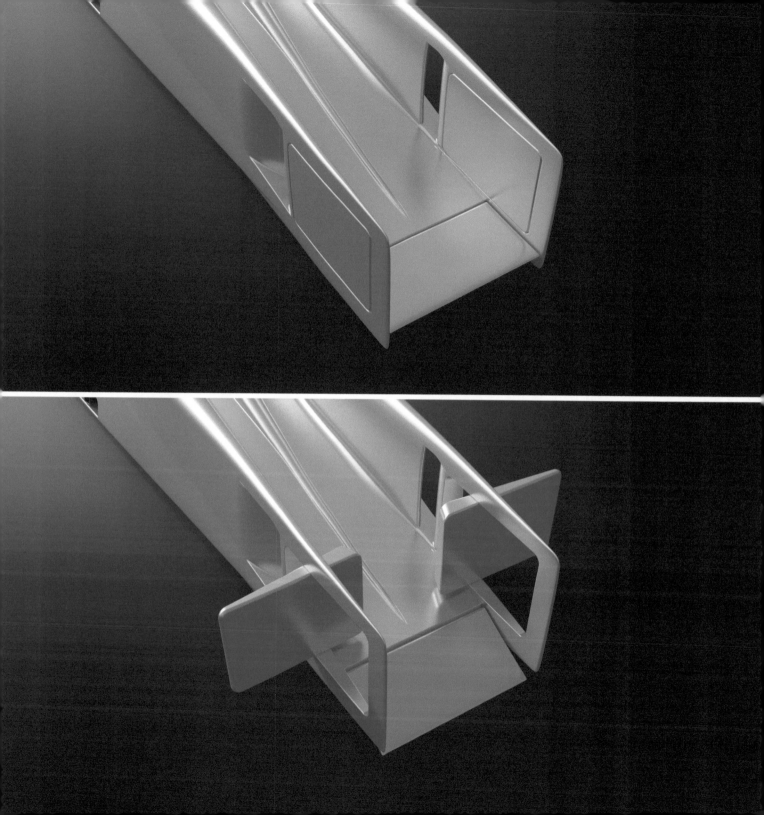

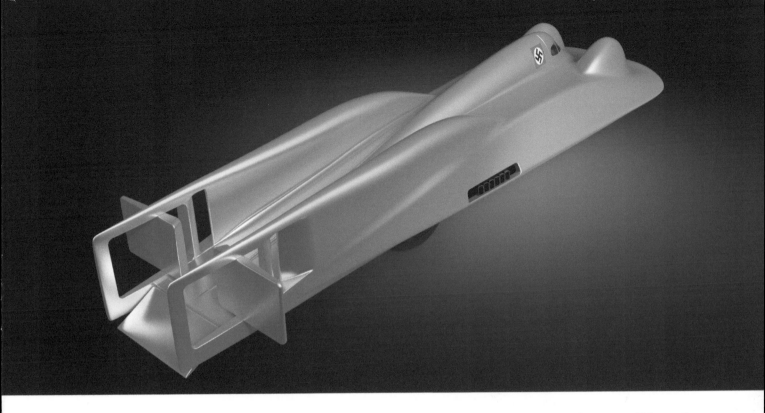

the drawings in patent no. 915,186, with cross sections borrowed and adapted from the earlier patent, no. 762,588. I assumed that the Sawatzki Record Car had the same overall tire diameter as the Mercedes-Benz T80—46.44 inches (1,180 mm). This resulted in a wheelbase of 194 inches (4,928 mm) and a track width

of 47.6 inches (1,209 mm). The overall length of the vehicle is estimated to be 389.3" (9,888 mm), or 32.44 ft (9.89 m), making it over six feet longer than the actual T80 as built. If this size is correct, the Sawatzki Record Car would have been one of the largest LSR vehicles of its era.

Like the T80, I assumed the Sawatzki Record Car was powered by the Daimler-Benz DB 603 engine, resulting in a similar arrangement and placement of the exhaust stacks. I also borrowed the spoked wheels, outline of the cockpit cover, and details of the interior from the T80.

The Sawatzki Record Car is painted silver overall with the Mercedes-Benz star on the nose. The swastika decal behind the cockpit is based on one applied to the Auto Union 6.3 liter *Stromlinienwagen* of 1937.

OPPOSITE: Closeup views of the tail of the Sawatzki Record Car. The top view shows the air brakes retracted and elevator in the neutral position, while the bottom view shows the air brakes deployed and elevator angled downwards to aid in rapidly stopping the vehicle at high speeds.

TOP: Rear view of the Sawatzki design with air brakes deployed and elevator angled downwards. Whether these devices would have been enough to slow the vehicle and prevent it from leaving the road surface at the end of its record run can only be speculated upon.

SIZE COMPARISON

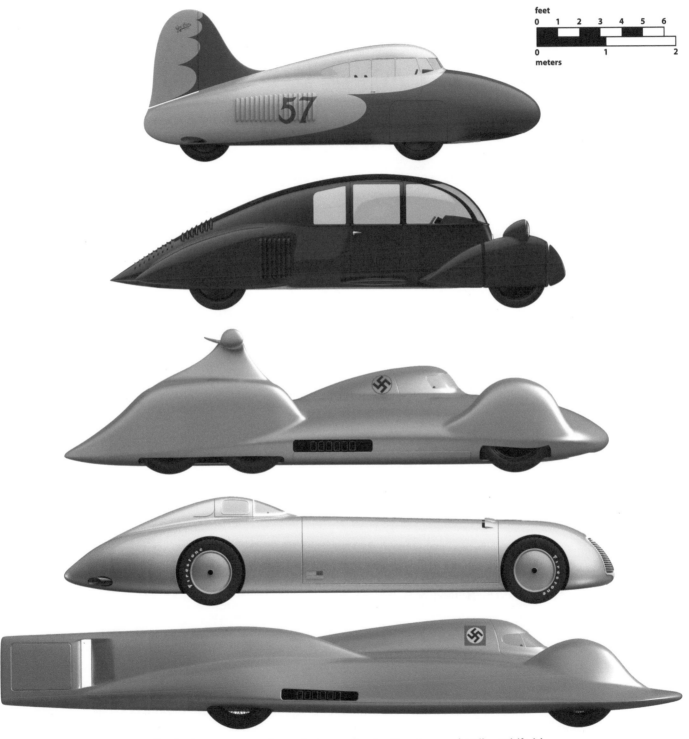

Note: All vehicle sizes are estimated, except for the Gee-Bee and Miller-Oldfield cars.

ENDNOTES AND BIBLIOGRAPHY

Endnotes

1. I lacked the rights to publish the image in this book, but you can view it online at http://theoldmotor. com/?p=124727, which also has some interesting background on Rystedt.

2. Accurate drawings and specifications of the original Opel RAK.2 proved elusive, so the overall tire diameter of Opel's official replica was used.

3. Dees, *The Miller Dynasty*, pp. 401—405B.

4. https://en.wikipedia.org/wiki/Barney_Oldfield

5. https://en.wikipedia.org/wiki/Harry_Miller_(auto_racing)

6. http://www.centennialofflight.net/essay/Explorers_Record_Setters_and_Daredevils/Gee_Bees/EX23.htm

7. Mendenhall, *The Gee Bee Racers: A Legacy of Speed*.

8. https://en.wikipedia.org/wiki/Mercedes-Benz_T80

9. https://de.wikipedia.org/wiki/Josef_Mickl

Bibliography

Dees, Mark L. *The Miller Dynasty: A Technical History of the Work of Harry A. Miller, His Associates, and His Successors*. Moorpark: The Hippodrome Publishing Co., 1994.

Mendenhall, Charles A. *The Gee Bee Racers: A Legacy of Speed*. North Park: Specialty Press, 1979.

Riedl, W.H.J. *Rocket Development with Liquid Propellants*. Derby: Rolls-Royce Heritage Trust, 2005.

Wayt, Hampton C. *Driving Through Futures Past: Mid-20th Century Automotive Design*. Los Angeles: Kythe Publishing Company, 2006.

Other Publications by Jared A. Zichek

Books from Retromechanix Productions
Available from Amazon.com & other booksellers

 Goodyear GA-28A/B *Convoy Fighter*: The Naval VTOL Turboprop Tailsitter Project of 1950 Forty illos of a bizarre competitor to the Convair Pogo & Lockheed Salmon; 34 pp. **Print $14.99/Digital $5.99**

 Martin Model 262 *Convoy Fighter*: The Naval VTOL Turboprop Project of 1950 Fifty-six illos of Martin's proposed rivals to the Convair Pogo & Lockheed Salmon; 52 pp. **Print $16.99/Digital $6.99**

 Northrop N-63 *Convoy Fighter*: The Naval VTOL Turboprop Tailsitter Project of 1950 Sixty-six illos of Northrop's handsome VTOL fighter proposals; 44 pp. **Print $15.99/Digital $6.49**

The American Aerospace Archive Magazine
Available at magcloud.com/user/jaredzichek

 1. Martin JRM Mars Flying Boat: Commercial Projects of 1944 Reproduction of a beautiful full color brochure for a civilian version of the world's largest flying boat; 36 pp. **Print $9.95/Digital $3.95**

 2. North American FJ-5 Fighter: A Navalized Derivative of the F-107A Five wind tunnel model photos and 28 drawings of North American's unusual 1955 proposal; 36 pp. **Print $9.95/Digital $3.95**

 3. The B-52 Competition of 1946...and Dark Horses from Douglas, 1947-1950 Seventy-seven rare images of early postwar strategic bomber projects; 60 pp. **Print $14.95/Digital $5.95**

 4. McDonnell Naval Jet Fighters: Selected Proposals and Mock-up Reports, 1945-1957 97 photos and drawings of early postwar jet fighter proposals & prototypes; 60 pp. **Print $14.95/Digital $5.95**

 5. Mother Ships, Parasites and More: Selected USAF Strategic Bomber, XC Heavy Transport and FICON Studies, 1945-1954 Composite aircraft projects; 258 illos; 204 pp. **Print $49.95/Digital $9.95**

Books from Schiffer Publishing
Available from Amazon.com & other booksellers

 The Boeing XF8B-1 Fighter: Last of the Line Hundreds of rare photos, drawings, artist's impressions and manual extracts covering Boeing's last piston engine fighter; 376 pp. **$45.59**

 Secret Aerospace Projects of the U.S. Navy: The Incredible Attack Aircraft of the USS United States, 1948-1949 Hundreds of rare photos and drawings; 232 pp. **$45.81**

Websites

 Retromechanix.com features hundreds of rare high resolution images and reports covering U.S. prototype and project aircraft from the 1930s through the 1950s. Many free and low cost digital downloads available!

Lightning Source UK Ltd.
Milton Keynes UK
UKHW051853011221
394889UK00002B/83